SWASTIKA OVER PARIS

SWASTIKA OVER PARIS

JEREMY JOSEPHS

With a foreword by
SERGE KLARSFELD

Arcade Publishing · New York
Little, Brown and Company

FIRST U.S. EDITION

ISBN 1-55970-036-X

Library of Congress Cataloging-in-Publication Information is available

Published in the United States by
Arcade Publishing Inc., New York,
a Little, Brown company

10   9   8   7   6   5   4   3   2   1

HC

PRINTED IN THE UNITED STATES OF AMERICA

FOR GEORGES-ANDRÉ KOHN

CONTENTS

Preface

I began research for this book by making contact with survivors'
groups and various other Jewish organizations in Paris. Rapidly,
one contact led to another. It was this peculiar and entirely
unplanned path which eventually led to Philippe Kohn and
Paulette Szlifke, neither of whom had the remotest notion of
my background or motives. Yet both immediately conferred
upon me the privilege of unconditional access to the detailed
stories of their lives, and in Philippe's case to that of his father
too. I shall always remain grateful to them for having opened
my eyes to the story of French Jewry during the Occupation.

Although their stories are but two among tens of thousands –
each one unique – it was never my intention to write an academic
tome describing in detail the history of the Holocaust in France.
Rather I wanted to produce an accessible personalized account of
the events and decrees initiated in Paris. Nevertheless, *Swastika
Over Paris* is a true account and every event referred to did indeed
take place. The only exception is the name of one individual, which
has been changed on the advice of my solicitor. Likewise, where
dialogue appears it is authentic. Every line has been checked to
the best of my ability, although needless to say any mistakes are
of my own making.

I had no idea of the scale of the project on which I had embarked.
The writing of *Swastika Over Paris* naturally entailed several visits
to France for research and interviews. Its preparation and writing
took almost four years. Although I have lived in France for several
periods, I must confess that I had little idea of the plight of French
Jewry during the Second World War. Drancy, *La Grande Rafle*, the
Vélodrome d'Hiver, were meaningless to me. I became convinced

that if I was ignorant of the story of Jewish suffering during the Occupation, then the chances were that others also were uninformed.

This book does not grind to a halt in 1945 with the end of the war. As you will learn from Serge Klarsfeld's Foreword, a number of campaigns are being fought at this very moment. In Syria today lives the man responsible for the suffering inflicted on both Paulette Szlifke and Philippe Kohn. Aloïs Brünner is the last major war criminal still at large and it is very much hoped that this book will give added impetus to the campaign to bring him to justice. In West Germany Arnold Strippel lives as a free man and receives a government pension, despite having meted out death and misery beyond all comprehension.

Many people helped me in the preparation of *Swastika Over Paris*, but in particular I would like to thank Mrs Christa Wichmann of the Institute of Contemporary History and Wiener Library; Vidar Jacobsen of the Centre de Documentation Juive Contemporaine in Paris; Haley and Victor Baneth for their help in the production of the typescript; my dear friend Jeff Lewis for his constructive editorial work; and my agent Michael Motley for having shared my enthusiasm for this project. Above all, though, I would like to thank my wife, Clair, for having put up with my grumpiness on the numerous occasions when I felt I was not making much headway.

Let me say, finally, that I am grateful to have learned about the atmosphere prevailing in the streets of Paris just fifty years ago. For, since Paulette Szlifke and Philippe Kohn are precisely the same age as my parents, it is most certainly true that 'there but for the Grace of God go I.'

Jeremy Josephs
Autumn 1989

Foreword

When Jeremy Josephs came to see me in Paris a few years ago
and showed me the outline of the book he was planning to write,
I tried to dissuade him. He is not part of the generation who knew
and experienced the persecution of Jews in the course of their own
lives, emotions and affections. What was more, he was not a French
Jew, and he did not live through that time of darkness and horror.
I thought he was unlikely to be able to reconstruct the tragedy of
these events and the moments that belong only to those who lived
through them personally.

But in *Swastika Over Paris*, Jeremy Josephs has amply risen to
the challenge of conveying the stark reality of:

- The Gestapo's persecution of the Jews, with the active col-
  lusion of the Vichy government's police and administration
  systems, aided by a formidable array of anti-Semitic laws.

- The French people's initial indifference to the plight of the
  Jews, followed by compassion in the summer of 1942 when
  they realized that the Jews being arrested, including old people
  and children, were being sent not into forced labour but to
  their deaths.

- The blindness of those French Jews who had been assimilated
  and thought they could be saved by feigning adherence to
  Nazism. They would undoubtedly not have survived on a
  large scale had it not been for timely victories by the Allies.
  But a number of Jews in this category still met their deaths: one
  sad example was Armand Kohn, director of the Rothschild

Hospital, who is one of the heroes of Jeremy Josephs' book. I am only too familiar with the plight of people like Kohn, being a friend of his surviving son, Philippe.

- The anguish of the stateless and foreign Jews who, with their French children, represented more than 85 per cent of the 80,000 victims of the Final Solution to the Jewish Question in France. This anguish turned into combative despair. There was the Jewish Resistance itself, which fought and tried to save Jewish lives, particularly those of children; and then there were the Jews who fought against the occupying power in a variety of other resistance movements. The Communist Jews were the most active of the latter. At the great trial of the 'terrorists' of *L'Affiche Rouge* in spring 1943, twelve of the 23 resistance fighters sentenced to death and executed were Jews. At Mont-Valérien, the shrine of the French Resistance, 160 of the thousand people shot were Jews: 16 per cent of the total, at a time when Jews made up only 0.7 per cent of the French population as a whole.

In Jeremy Josephs' book, it is the young, heroic Paulette Szlifke who strikingly embodies both the Jewish Resistance itself and more general resistance by the Jews.

Jeremy Josephs portrays not only the victims, but also the fanaticism, drive, cunning and cruelty of the oppressor: Aloïs Brünner, Eichmann's right-hand man, who was sent on a mission to France to deport as many Jews as possible from this difficult hunting ground.

Brünner became Camp Commandant at Drancy, the antechamber of death, where Jews were assembled before being transported to Auschwitz. Both camps, with all their evil memories, provide the setting for the book, along with the old Jewish quarters of Paris and the Rothschild hospital which all the main figures in the book pass through. Brünner: I know him well, and yet I have never seen him. A thin plywood partition was all that stood between him and me that night of September 30, 1943, when he and a team of Austrian SS men broke into our apartment in Nice to arrest us, taking advantage of the departure of the Italians who had previously provided ample protection for the Jews. My father had hidden us behind the false back of a cupboard: my mother, my sister, and myself aged eight. I can still hear the Gestapo officer's voice when my father opened the door: 'Where are your wife and children?' I can still hear them searching the apartment, trying to find us, and I will never forget the screams of our friends, the little Jewish girls next door, who were beaten by the Gestapo to force their parents to reveal where their eldest son was hidden. All of them, my father included, were murdered in Auschwitz. As for Brünner, my wife and I tracked him down in Damascus in 1982. I was expelled from Syria, followed by my wife in 1987, but we managed to persuade first Germany and then France to apply for his extradition from Syria. There have not been any results so far, but we are not giving up, nor will we as long as there is breath in our bodies. Brünner is now an oppressor protected by another oppressor: Syria itself is holding its last 5,000 Jews to ransom.

Jeremy Josephs' book gives a great deal more weight to the events of the Final Solution. It is now nearly half a century since they happened, but their repercussions are still being felt today. Philippe Kohn is still suffering the agonies Brünner inflicted on him; Paulette Szlifke is still setting an example as a militant. Aloïs Brünner regrets none of the crimes he perpetrated against the Jews, 'those creatures of the Devil,' as he calls them, and has said he would do it all again. We are still busy ourselves: now that we have unmasked Lischka and Barbie, and brought them to trial, we will do our best to make sure Brünner is next. As for Jeremy Josephs, this book makes him part of the generation of people who have taken on the job of keeping these events alive in all our memories. It is a book that is full of life and death, a big book which is laden with events and suffering, recounted with skill and passion. Jeremy Josephs' book will help to continue our struggle into the twenty-first century. He was right not to have followed the advice I first gave him.

Serge Klarsfeld

1

La Grande Peur

A few weeks earlier it would have been unthinkable. A few months earlier it would have been laughable. The idea that German troops were poised to stage a victory parade along the entire length of the Champs-Élysées was preposterous. Yet now the unthinkable, the laughable and the preposterous had all but come about. Paris was on the brink of occupation.

The fighting was almost over. Not that there had been much by way of battle. The Maginot Line, meticulously devised to protect France from all those with designs upon her, had simply been bypassed. It was not that André Maginot had not served a useful purpose. He had. Indeed, his protective shield was more than just a feat in engineering terms: it was nothing less than the pride of the entire nation. The problem with the Maginot Line was relatively simple: it was in the wrong place. German troops had done what should surely have been obvious even to the rawest military recruit: they had attacked from an altogether different direction.

The unhappy consequences were now there for all to see. The capital of France was declared an open city. Official papers were burned, official buildings abandoned. Government officials were themselves on the run, as everyone from Prime Minister to factory worker began frantic preparations to leave the city. Following the Government's failure in battle, its sole contribution was to turn from matters military to matters spiritual, hastily convening a Mass at the Cathedral of Notre-Dame. The holy relics of Saint

15

Geneviève and Saint Louis were paraded, as if in a last-ditch attempt to ward off the quickening pace of the German advance.

Panic engulfed the city. *La Grande Peur* – the great fear – swept like a tidal wave through the boulevards of the capital. The exodus had begun. Between one fifth and a quarter of the population took to the roads. Some were strafed and bombarded by German aircraft, whose pilots sensed that victory could be only moments away.

It was a migration of fear. Parisians gathered their most precious possessions, at least those they could carry. And they left, their destination unknown. The priority was simple: not to be caught in the capital. The main roads of the city, the *routes nationales*, were soon overloaded with traffic. People appeared to be running everywhere, nervous ants scurrying in every direction. Homes were deserted, offices abandoned.

One eyewitness described the flight from Paris in these terms:

Along the entire length of the Boulevard Saint-Michel, an uninterrupted flow of people began to leave Paris with the most varied means of transport. Cars crammed with luggage; heavy trucks loaded with people and suitcases. Some set out on bicycles, others proceeded at a more modest pace, pushing small hand-carts, with the occasional dog to be seen here and there tied underneath on a lead. Huge country carts were proceeding as fast as two or three plough-horses could manage, loaded with bales of hay. On the edge of the pavements stood a number of people with cases, their faces blending bewilderment with despair, waiting for transport of every conceivable kind, whilst the more fortunate crammed as much into their cars as possible. At the Boulevard Saint-Germain it was much the same spectacle. In the rue Dauphine luggage was strewn all over the pavements. Trucks loaded up. Shops shut up. Others were preparing to leave with nothing more elaborate than a pram.

While some were fleeing to escape the ravages of war, others hoped one day to be mobilized to recapture the city they loved. A run on the banks ensued as people clamoured to withdraw their savings. In June of 1940 the banks returned to their customers some 1,212 million francs.

Amid the chaos of this mass exodus ninety thousand children were separated from their parents. A few days later, the provincial press was full of small ads which indicated the scale of the suffering:

> Madame Cissé, refugeed in Loupiac-de-Cadillac, seeks her three children, Hélène, Simone and Jean – lost at St Pierre-des-Corps, June 15. Box number.

Some families would be reunited. Others not. Many thousands, both young and old, were to perish in the frantic flight from Paris.

The great city was disintegrating. Deserted and silent, without traffic, Métro or radio. And as quickly as the population vacated the capital, so the Germans advanced. On Friday, June 14 the German High Command published the following communiqué:

> As a result of the total collapse of the entire French front between the Channel and the Maginot Line near Montmédy the French High Command has abandoned its original intention of defending the French capital. While this communiqué is being broadcast victorious German troops are entering Paris.

And so they were. Paris had fallen. The previous evening two French negotiators, Commander Devouges and Lieutenant Holtzer, together with a trumpeter, had held a secret rendezvous with a German captain in front of the Town Hall at Sarcelles, a few kilometres to the north of Paris. It was agreed that the capital would not be defended, but handed over with due process and according to international convention. Within moments French signatures appeared at the base of the surrender document. In any event, apart from the sandbags surrounding the Eiffel Tower and various other of the nation's proud monuments, there was little evidence of any attempt to defend the city. So the great battle for Paris never took place. Only one courageous French colonel, with a handful of men, attempted anything remotely resembling resistance by establishing a machine-gun post towards the north of the city.

The troops of von Kuchler's XVIIIth army entered Paris by the Porte de la Villette on June 14 at 05.30 hours, thirty-six days after the offensive had begun on the Dutch frontier. Two formations advanced. As dawn approached, one headed towards the Eiffel Tower and the other towards the Arc de Triomphe. Before midday General Bogislav von Studnitz, the first commandant of 'Greater Paris,' had taken up his quarters at the Hôtel Crillon, known for its extravagant décor, and in one of the plushest areas of the city. Everything went according to plan.

Denied the opportunity to fight for their city, several Parisians chose to take their own lives, the Mayor of Clichy among them. But neither suicides nor sandbags could stop the Germans from savouring the moment of their historic triumph. It had not been a battle so much as a walk-over. Time now to celebrate. And for the Germans, there was only one place in which to do so – the Champs-Élysées. As the victorious troops paraded up and down the most famous avenue in France, the Arc de Triomphe had never looked more incongruous.

Only the eighty-four-year-old Marshal Pétain had been warning that France could be invaded if she ignored Germany's expansionary ambitions. But his words had gone unheeded. When France awoke to the spectacle of German troops pouring into the capital, it was too late. But it came as no surprise that the country should look to its ageing hero-warrior from the First World War to provide the inspiration, vision and leadership of which his successors had evidently been so completely devoid.

For Pétain, the war was over. The exodus from Paris had convinced him of the futility of any resistance. He was asked to form a government. If only the French generals had waged war as smoothly as they now sought peace. For within hours of taking office the hero of Verdun was pleading with the Germans for an armistice. His first act as head of state was to summon the

Spanish Ambassador, Felix de Lequerica, requesting him to use his good offices to ascertain Hitler's terms for an armistice. Lequerica telephoned two attachés waiting at St Jean-de-Luz. They walked across the Franco-Spanish frontier and from Irún passed on to the Germans in Madrid Pétain's plea for an armistice. The Germans' terms were in fact relatively modest; at least when compared with those that other conquered nations had been obliged to accept.

France was to be divided in two. The southern region, approximately two-fifths of the country, would constitute the *zone non-occupée*, or unoccupied France. This would serve as the seat of the Government of France, with its headquarters in Vichy, to be led by Marshal Pétain himself. All French territory came under the jurisdiction of Vichy law so long as such laws were consistent with German regulations. That was the good news. The Government of France would go on. The less attractive part of the package was the inevitable: the remainder of France was to be placed under the authority of the German commanding officer for Belgium and Northern France. Naturally, this region would include Paris. The two *départements* of Nord and Pas de Calais would constitute this 'zone occupée.' Alsace and a large part of Lorraine were annexed outright by Germany. That was one old score settled; the actual signing of the armistice treaty on June 22 was to provide the setting for another.

The time had come for a little bit of theatrics, to which the Führer was by no means averse. In the forest of Compiègne, some fifty kilometres north-east of Paris, Adolf Hitler was busy preparing an elaborate humiliation for the French. The same railway carriage in which Marshal Ferdinand Foch had dictated the terms of the armistice to the German generals when they had surrendered after the First World War was to be dusted down and used again. With the carriage still a national monument in France, there could hardly have been a more perfect stage on which to humiliate the French. The scene was to be re-enacted with the roles reversed.

Hitler was having a field day. Standing outside the carriage and smiling broadly, he stamped his foot with deep satisfaction. It was all filmed for consumption in the Reich. The British propaganda film service edited the sequence to make it appear as though a demented Hitler was dancing a bizarre jig of Austrian origin. In fact, this day and this occasion were the apotheosis of his military career. Hitler was hailed as the greatest field commander of all time, his strategic vision fully vindicated. After the ceremony the German top brass returned to their field headquarters in the village of Bruly.

There was more to come. Hitler now wanted to see his much-cherished prize, Paris – the jewel in the crown of the Greater Reich. Very early the next morning, he flew to the French capital. It was the familiar tourist's itinerary. A fleet of cars sped past the Arc de Triomphe, Avenue Foch, Trocadéro, the Eiffel Tower, the German Embassy, Notre-Dame and most of the famous sights of Paris. During the course of this impromptu tour, Hitler had spotted the statue of General Mangin, another of France's First World War commanders. Three days later it was levelled. Yet apparently overwhelmed by the beauty of Paris, the Führer said:

I am grateful to fate – to have seen this town whose aura has always preoccupied me. At the beginning of hostilities I gave orders to the troops to find a way around Paris and to avoid fighting in its periphery. For it is our responsibility at several levels to preserve undamaged this wonder of Western civilisation. We have succeeded.

Hitler returned to Berlin, amply satisfied with his new and glittering prize.

For the vast majority of French citizens the armistice came as a relief. As General de Gaulle was later to recall, 'not a single public figure raised his voice to condemn the armistice.' It seemed as if the war was over. Now, life had to go on.

And it did. Some trembled at their first sight of a German officer. Others buried their heads in shame. But by far the most common reaction to the arrival of the swarms of Germans in Paris was to conclude that there appeared to be little cause for concern. As one popular paper asked, were not the German soldiers 'handsome boys, decent, helpful and above all correct'? At least order had been restored. Before the German invasion, the city had been slowly grinding to a halt. Now the opposite was true: with Germans in control, the Métro was working again. The banks and post offices had reopened. True, the clocks had moved forward one hour to coincide with the time of the Greater Reich — but so what?

Germans flocked to the Lido Club on the Champs-Élysées and to the other celebrated night spots of the city. Barely a fortnight after the signing of the armistice, Paris appeared to be back in full swing. The schools were back. The Opera was back. The Jockey Club was back. Everything was back. Paris was still 'Gai Paris,' no matter who controlled her. The city had changed hands but had apparently emerged unscathed from the ordeal. Most of the same faces were in the same places. Maurice Chevalier would come into town from time to time, to sing on Radio-Paris: unmistakably the voice of France.

Caviar could still be bought. Women could still be bought, with the city's most famous brothel 'One Two Two' reporting an increased turnover. Paris was still the place to be. Consequently, many prominent Germans felt obliged to have their interests represented in the French capital. As Hitler himself put it, Paris had become a German Babylon — everyone's favourite resort.

Yet the city was undergoing a slow metamorphosis. German sign-posts appeared everywhere. A microcosm of the Reich was gradually taking shape. Certain cinemas and theatres were converted into Soldatenkinos, for the exclusive use of the occupying troops. A German bookshop opened here, a German canteen there. Before long the city was covered with that unmistakable symbol of the Reich, the swastika. Indeed, the Chambre des Députés was awash with them. And as if the message was not clear enough, an enormous banner was draped across the building. 'Deutschland siegt an allen Fronten,' it declared — 'Germany is victorious on all Fronts.' Nobody could argue with that.

So Paris was the same, but only superficially. In fact, its character had changed. Gone was the Paris with a reputation for tolerance and compassion. A new and ominous philosophy had been imported. On the same day that German troops had entered the city, the Gestapo had arrived as well. Not that anyone knew it. They were a small group of about twenty men, who wore the uniform of the Secret Military Police. Passing completely unnoticed in their unmarked cars, which bore only military number plates, these men had come to Paris to execute the will of the Nazi Party, to convert Nazi theory into Parisian practice. France's turn had come. That very first evening the undercover group registered at the Hôtel du Louvre. Early next morning it set to work. Its first visit was to the Prefecture of Police. One member set off and demanded a number of dossiers on political opponents of the Reich. The relevant files were ready and waiting.

The leader of that Sonderkommando was Helmut Knochen. He had been selected by Reinhard Heydrich himself in Berlin. Tall and presentable and barely thirty years old, Knochen was one of the young rising stars of the Nazi Party. He had already shown an exceptional capacity for organization and decision-making. His career prospects were considerably enhanced because of his role in the Venlo affair, in which he had distinguished himself by kidnapping two British intelligence officers. Everyone knew the name of Helmut Knochen – the athlete, the intellectual, the linguist, the cultured, polished man with such an agreeable manner. The Paris posting was his reward. Knochen could do no wrong, the Iron Cross First and Second Class having been hastily conferred upon him, and he was given carte blanche to pick a team of aides to accompany him to the French capital.

Helmut Knochen was born on March 14, 1910 at Magdeburg. His father, Karl, was a schoolteacher who went out of his way to ensure that his son received a strict, disciplined education similar to his own. An industrious pupil, Helmut studied at the Universities of Leipzig, Halle and Göttingen before obtaining his doctorate in 1935. His choice of subject was well removed from the field of political intelligence. For he produced a thesis on the English playwright George Coleman. In fact Helmut's ambition was to teach literature – but his father had already enrolled him in the youth section of the Stahlhelm, which embarked on a long and violent nationalist campaign. By the time the Nazis had come to power it had become increasingly difficult to graduate unless one belonged to one of the Party organizations. In 1933 Knochen joined the Nazi Party.

An alternative career was beginning to emerge. At first he dabbled in journalism, but soon his articles began to appear in the *Studentenpresse*, an organ of the Ministry for Culture. For Knochen, writing was proving to be both more enjoyable and more remunerative than a professorship, and in 1936 he abandoned his studies to enter the Deutsches Nachrichten Büro, the official press agency of the Nazi Party. At the age of twenty-six he had become its editor. It was in this capacity that he attended the Olympic Games in Berlin in 1936, renewing contact with one of his former professors, Dr Six, who had also left academia for the Sicherheitsdienst (Security Service), the Press Section of which he now ran. Knochen and Six had much in common. Soon they were working together, Knochen having entered the SD's main offices in Berlin where he was given the rank of SS-Obersturmführer.

One of Knochen's first tasks in Berlin had been to prepare a detailed study of the French, Belgian and Dutch presses. Thus, when he was despatched to Paris as leader of the Sonderkommando, he already had some understanding of the nature of French society and politics, in addition to speaking the language. He had even visited Paris in 1937 to see the Exhibition. His understanding of Paris and the French was such that he seemed the perfect choice, and no one in Berlin seriously questioned his appointment.

Despite his position in the Nazi Party, Knochen retained the looks of a Doctor of Philosophy. Anyone anticipating the arrival in Paris of a political hoodlum was to be disappointed. But as some Parisians would eventually discover, his appearance, wit and culture were to prove no impediment to his execution of his work.

The Knochen Kommando continued to organize rapidly. No time could be wasted when dealing with enemies of the Reich. There were anti-Nazi German and Austrian refugees in the city, and Freemasons and Communists too. The offices of all suspects would have to be closed, their records seized and houses searched. And, of course, there were the Jews.

What fate awaited the Jews of Paris now that Knochen and the SD had established this first foothold in the city? The first clue came some weeks later, on September 27, 1940, with the publication by the German authorities of the 'First Ordinance.' The target had to be defined: Who was a Jew? The Ordinance provided the answer: 'all those who belong, or used to belong, to the Jewish religion, or who have more than two grandparents who are Jewish.'

The principal point of the Ordinance, however, was to announce that a census of Jews was to be taken. All Jews were instructed to report to the Prefecture of Police before October 20. A declaration made by the head of a family would suffice for the family as a whole. Exactly 149,734 Parisian Jews duly subscribed. Point Four of the Ordinance obliged all Jewish-owned businesses to put up a sign in their premises indicating Jewish ownership – in both German and French, so that there could be no doubt. Notices reading 'Entreprise Juive' and 'Jüdisches Geschäft' sprang up all over the city, especially in the eleventh and twelfth *arrondissements*, the ancient Jewish quarters of Paris. This First Ordinance was considered by many to be a fairly mild document. Registers and stickers. The Germans and their lists. There was really little cause for concern. So much for the persecution of the Jews.

2

More French than the French

For the majority of Parisians the great exodus from the city had been an overwhelmingly traumatic affair. For the Kohn family, however, it was an altogether more civilized departure. It was simply a question of foresight. Foresight and money. Armand Kohn had an abundant supply of both. For when war was declared between France and Germany, he immediately saw the writing on the wall. Indeed, the general assumption was that with Paris on the brink of bombardment, there was little point in waiting to see precisely who would survive the onslaught.

The Kohns were off. But they saw no good reason why their retreat from Paris should not be distinctly stylish. Everything the Kohns had ever done was carried out with considerable finesse. The family would simply drive to their holiday home in Deauville, the seaside town long known as France's premier playground for the rich and pampered. To avoid any undue hardship, and ensure that their needs would be catered to, the family's loyal maid Patricia would accompany them. While thousands of less fortunate Parisians continued their miserable exodus towards the South, the Kohns leisurely drove to their villa, sipping cold drinks en route. They arrived to find the rooms the same as ever. It seemed like just another exciting summer holiday.

For Philippe Kohn, Armand's fourteen-year-old and eldest son, this was no ordinary outing. For unlike on all previous visits, there was apparently no fixed date for returning to Paris. Here, then, was the perfect treat, an endless holiday by the sea. Enrolled in the local high school, Philippe was in no doubt: he was having the time of his life.

Armand Kohn had never devoted much energy to political issues.

He was a businessman, a banker by profession. But he did like to keep abreast of all developments relating to the war because of the numerous commercial implications. When he learned that German troops had swept through Belgium and were poised to enter France, he decided that even gentle Deauville was too close for comfort, and prepared to leave for the Basque country, well away from the battles raging to the north. It was another delightful spot. Armand had been invited to bring the family to stay with his aunt, Nadine Thierry, who lived in the picturesque town of Guéthary, situated between Biarritz and St Jean-de-Luz, only moments from the Spanish border.

Nadine Thierry had married Philippe de Rothschild, and so had joined the most prominent Jewish family in France. The Kohn family had barely installed themselves with their hosts, when news filtered through that Paris had fallen. The city had not been bombarded as Armand had earlier feared. Philippe de Rothschild had assumed that the Kohns were fleeing from France. *He* certainly was. He explained to Armand Kohn that the Third Reich could hardly have been more explicit in its intentions towards the Jews. Therefore, he announced, the Rothschilds would shortly be leaving France, despite the fact that they were acknowledged spokesmen for, and a symbol of, French Jewry.

The Kohns, though, would not be going. They became regular visitors to the Spanish border, but only to bid farewell to relatives and friends. Time and again the scene repeated itself. Furious wavings, generally followed by tears. After these painful partings, the Kohn family would return to their new home in the Basque country. Armand Kohn had decided that his family was going to remain in France. In fact, not only were the Kohns to remain in France, they would shortly be returning to the capital. The entire family was to return to Paris.

Armand Eduard Kohn was a Jew, although in truth he really felt more French than Jewish. Unlike the Rothschilds, who had been obliged to take a higher profile on Jewish issues, Armand Kohn was a good deal more discreet about his Jewishness. He was a Frenchman through and through, in many respects more

French than the French. His was no immigrant family fleeing from a pogrom in Poland, but one of the grand old Jewish families of France. They had assimilated almost completely. In fact, Armand's was at least the seventh generation of Kohns in France. And unlike many of the new Jewish settlers, who often retained a ghetto mentality, the Kohns had long moved in the most sophisticated and celebrated of circles.

Nor had Armand been shy to fight for his country, albeit within the ranks of the British army during the First World War. He was badly gassed in the trenches by the Germans, and his condition had deteriorated during a prolonged period of captivity. From then on, Armand Kohn always suffered from various respiratory ailments. Over the years, he had visited a number of mountain resorts, hoping to benefit from the clearer air. He boasted an enviable war record, having been awarded the *Croix des Combatants* and the *Médaille de la Reconnaissance Française*, neither of which was conferred lightly. The old *invalide de guerre* had been profoundly affected by his experiences during that great war and had spent long hours telling his four children about them. His reminiscences served only to deepen and reinforce his strong feelings of nationalism and loyalty towards France.

Armand Kohn was of the old school: a Frenchman and proud of it. It was inconceivable to leave France, to abandon his beloved country just because the going happened to be rough. That would have been cowardice of the worst kind and he would have no part of it.

While the Kohns had assimilated and integrated, and were as aristocratic as any well-to-do Catholic family, they never sought to disguise their Jewishness. Before the outbreak of war, Armand had often taken Philippe and his younger brother Georges-André to the old synagogue in the rue de la Victoire in the ninth *arrondissement*, to attend the Sabbath service. It was a rather ambiguous sort of Jewishness though, Armand broadly believing in the faith while singularly failing to practise even its most elementary of rituals. The Highest Holy Days in the Jewish calendar, Rosh Hashanah and Yom Kippur, were respected, but not observed in earnest.

The ancient dietary laws of Kashrut were regularly flouted, with pork making more than the occasional appearance on the family dinner table. There were no mezuzahs, with their tightly folded parchment scrolls, to mark as Jewish the entrance of the Kohn home; nor traditional Friday-night meals to herald the arrival of the Sabbath. Once Armand and the boys emerged from Synagogue any notion of piety was promptly discarded. The Sabbath may have included a brief interlude of prayer, but it was seldom observed as a holy day of rest in the Kohn household.

In other respects Armand Kohn was a particular and methodical man. He liked routine and respected order. Never more at ease than when in a large post office, he adored the complexities of its organization, with people scurrying about, preparing, posting, sending and stamping. He went out of his way to ensure that he always carried no fewer than five differently coloured pens in his jacket, each one for a particular purpose intelligible only to him.

This ability to organize and be precise had served his banking interests well, for in that world he was a respected figure known for his meticulous efficiency and dedication. However, these qualities also lent themselves to a stubbornness of character. Indeed, Armand Kohn was a man who took pride in the rigidity of his views. The position could hardly have been clearer: once he had decided upon a strategy, nothing could make him change his mind. The strategy was entirely honourable: it was to preserve the unity of the family. Kohn believed that this could be accomplished as well in Paris as anywhere else in the world. The fact that Knochen and his bridgehead had by now consolidated their earlier foothold in the city appeared not to deter him at all.

Before long, Armand Kohn had said it so many times that it had begun to take on the air of a well-worn advertising slogan. No one actually believed it, but that did not prevent its constant repetition:

So long as we stay together, nothing can possibly happen to us. I'm a wounded war veteran. I have fought for my country. We have nothing to fear. As long as we do what is asked of us, no harm can come.

With the publication of the First Ordinance, Armand promptly went along to the local Commissaire of Police to register as required of him in his capacity as *chef de famille*. Here was the essence of Armand Kohn's secret strategy: he would acknowledge, respect, carry out and implement whatever the occupying forces demanded of him. And the reason for this high level of co-operation? Because he had nothing whatsoever to hide. Armand Kohn would never be seen to run. He would not simply pack his bags and go; or hide. Rules were rules, however unpalatable. Armand Kohn had never broken a rule in his life and he had no intention of doing so now.

Relatives and friends, astonished at Kohn's decision to return and remain in Paris, regularly pleaded with him to leave. They argued that one need not be an expert in political intelligence to realize that things were going to get a lot worse for the Jews.

Decrees and promulgations were formulated almost daily. But each time the subject of leaving arose, Armand would launch into the familiar litany regarding his decision to remain in Paris. In fact, so adamant was he in his resolve to stay that the Kohns became known as *les volontaires de la mort* – the volunteers of death. This cruel jibe served only to strengthen Armand's determination not to run. Anyone could run. It was far more difficult and delicate a task to succeed in Paris, a city now firmly in the grip of the Reich.

When young Philippe went into hiding in a farm outside of Paris, in an attempt to rid himself of his new nickname with its macabre implications, Armand tracked him down, and made him return to Paris, where he promptly despatched him to the local Commissaire of Police to ensure that his papers were in order. Later, when Philippe spoke of joining the Free French Forces in Africa under General de Gaulle, Armand locked his son in his room for eight days in the hope that it might make him see sense. Armand was a tender jailer, though, returning every day from his office at midday to take his son some lunch. But no lunch would be complete without another stern lecture. Seldom did the words vary:

You will not leave this house. Hiding like that. Talking of leaving us. You'll have on your conscience the death of the entire family.

Armand's wife Suzanne was by no means happy with the decision to remain in Paris. She too had spent long hours pleading with her husband to leave the country while they still could. And like so many others she too had received the same old answer: 'So long as we stay together, nothing can happen to us.' Unlike her son, though, Suzanne Kohn accepted what Armand said. She would never have contemplated anything else. In any event, this pattern of adhering to the decisions of the *chef de famille* was one which was deeply familiar to her from her own upbringing.

Like Armand, Suzanne had been born into one of the most prominent Jewish families in France, in her case the Netres. Her father had had a brilliant academic career, coming first in the prestigious Polytechnique examinations, after which he had gone on to establish a highly successful tobacco factory. Like the Kohns, the Netres were established and integrated into French society. In the mid-nineteenth century an ancestor of Suzanne's had received a medal from Queen Victoria for bravery. And in the First World War Suzanne's brother, Roger, had died at the age of nineteen, a hero who had sacrificed his life fighting for France's independence from Germany.

Suzanne grew up in the elegant drawing-rooms of the capital's sixteenth and seventeenth *arrondissements*. Her grandparents boasted as a close friend Albert I of Monaco, the King of Monte Carlo, and often cruised with the royal family on the yacht *L'Hirondelle*. Suzanne enjoyed the good things in life: her *toilette*, good clothes and the fine arts. She was an extremely elegant woman whose striking appearance turned heads in high society.

Suzanne occupied herself with running the family apartment in La Muette, near the Bois de Boulogne. The Kohns lived on the fifth floor at 2 rue d'Andigne, one of the most prestigious addresses in Paris. Suzanne's world consisted of golf and horses, embroidery and music, and long hours reading the classics over a cup of hot chocolate, snugly tucked away in her rooms with their heavy damask hangings. The music of Handel, Bach and Mozart were seldom far away, and the atmosphere in the Kohn household was always one of elegance and ease.

Yet something tugged at the conscience of Suzanne Kohn. While not in a position to challenge her husband's decision, she felt there might nonetheless be other avenues to explore. If the Germans were indeed to embark upon a campaign of persecution of the Jews, then the children should convert to Catholicism. It was a familiar ploy. A sympathetic priest was found, a few lessons were learned, a few francs changed hands, and four certificates of Catholicism followed without undue delay or devotion. Five certificates, in fact, for Suzanne converted too. Armand was initially opposed to the idea, but when he realized that this might assist in his campaign for family unity, he reluctantly agreed. One thing was certain, however: Armand would not convert.

Like Armand, Suzanne had never been a pious Jew. While she had insisted that Philippe celebrate his bar mitzvah in July, 1936, the affair was not primarily spiritual in nature. Rather, it provided her with a perfect excuse to throw one of her extravagant parties, for which she enjoyed a considerable reputation. At the old synagogue in the rue Copernic, Philippe duly recited a portion of the law drawn from ancient Jewish scripture, but the primary business of the day was without doubt the party at La Muette, where over one hundred people were wined and dined. With well over half the guests not of Jewish stock, it was a wonderful atmosphere of multi-cultural assimilation, a truly French bar mitzvah.

Suzanne Kohn barely knew the meaning of anti-Semitism, at least not in personal terms. Certainly she was aware that anti-Semitism was by no means new to France. Indeed, in certain quarters of French society, hatred of the Jews was a well-established tradition long before the Germans arrived. With the Dreyfus case less than a century behind her, France exhibited a relatively high level of anti-Semitism. But the philosophy which the Germans imported along with their troops was wholly alien even by French standards. Occasional and mild discrimination was one thing,

31

the doctrine of National Socialism quite another. Armand Kohn consistently refused to distinguish one from the other.

Armand Kohn was simply unable or unwilling to accept the fact that the Jews of Paris and the occupying Nazis would not be able to peacefully coexist. The provisions of the First Ordinance may have been fairly mild, but they were by definition only the beginning of a process. When the Second Ordinance was published, on October 18, 1940, it concerned Armand in a most direct manner. It was another set of definitions and restrictions. From that date onwards, hardly one hundred days since the occupation of the city, various business activities were proscribed to the Jews. At the top of this list was banking. Armand's profession was henceforth a 'Jewish business activity' and thus illegal. Kohn was obliged to go to the Prefecture of Police, once again armed with the necessary paperwork, to declare himself and register anew.

Although depressed by this turn of events, Armand Kohn was nonetheless soon encouraged by what struck him as an interesting proposition. Now that the Rothschilds had left France, an administrator was required to head the Rothschild Hospital, the foremost Jewish hospital in France. As the closest, indeed the only, relative of the Rothschilds who had elected to remain in France, Armand Kohn was asked if he would take the job. It was pointed out to him that since the publication of the Second Ordinance, he was no longer able to continue with his banking activities. Here was something to do. Something, moreover, which could be of enormous benefit to the community. And as Armand soon realized, here was a new and compelling peg on which he could hang his decision to remain in Paris. And the best news of all? The entire family would be guaranteed safe passage in Paris. Armand Kohn accepted.

The job at the Rothschild Hospital came as a considerable relief to everyone, for the atmosphere in the Kohn household had become extremely tense. The children felt particularly frustrated as restriction after restriction was introduced. The Kohns' eldest daughter, seventeen-year-old Rose-Marie, was particularly upset because she felt that she was frittering away good years and good times. Without doubt, the greatest irritant was the eight o'clock curfew. Sometimes she and Philippe would leave home without permission and when they came home they were greeted with reproaches and recriminations. Sometimes there were occasional surprise parties with friends; anything to relieve the tension. At times Armand Kohn would work himself into a rage, declaring that his children had no right to be out after hours, which caused tempers to flare and tears to flow. The curfew *must* be obeyed for fear of terrible consequences. It was their father's familiar refrain, but one that the children found increasingly difficult to follow. Armand preached the necessity for family unity, but as 1940 drew to a close, the Kohn family was anything but unified.

As the Kohns continued to squabble, the Germans were in their heyday. With the New Year approaching, a magnificent party was being prepared at the German Embassy in Paris. No coupons or ration-cards here. Indeed, the buffet could hardly have been more lavish; every delicacy to be had in Paris was available. For the German top brass it was a superb evening. Suzanne and Armand Kohn were themselves well acquainted with the extravagances of glittering embassy occasions, but those days now appeared to be over. As the Germans danced, laughed and celebrated, the Kohns remained at home, unable to recall a more sorrowful entry into the New Year.

3

72 Avenue Foch

During the night of October 2, 1941, hundreds of Parisians were awakened from their sleep by a series of mysterious explosions around the city. At 2.30 am, an explosive device was detonated in the rue des Tourelles. An hour later another charge went off in the rue Notre-Dame-de-Nazareth. Shortly before daybreak there was a third huge detonation, this time in the rue de la Victoire, which showered glass everywhere. And so it went on through the early hours as three more streets trembled on their foundations. The six explosions shared only one common characteristic: each was designed to devastate a Jewish house of worship. The fuse of a seventh bomb failed to ignite, a fact which was interpreted by some religious Jews in the area as a sign that the Almighty had intervened on their behalf. Their joy was short-lived, however, for their ancient place of prayer was blown up the following day. The official report explained that this seventh act of sacrilege had been carried out for 'safety reasons.'

Here at last was incontrovertible evidence that the French really did hate the Jews. Finally, a spontaneous pogrom in Paris. Not at all. The 'pogrom' had been staged by the Nazis, just as the *Kristallnacht* of November 1938 had been made to look like a native uprising against German Jewry. It was an amateurish but deadly attempt to arouse public opinion in Paris. Behind it lay the hand of Helmut Knochen.

The attacks on the seven synagogues occurred sixteen months after the occupation of Paris. By now Helmut Knochen was well established in the French capital. In sole charge of the Gestapo-SD in France, he commanded the best officers in town. Moving from the Hôtel du Louvre, he eventually settled for 72 Avenue Foch, a stone's throw from the Arc de Triomphe. Additional premises were located at numbers 82 and 84, just a few yards further along. Avenue Foch was now clearly synonymous with the SD and the Gestapo. Their branches and substations had spread rapidly throughout the city. Swarms of armed guards, dozens of garages and fleets of shining black cars were there for all to see.

Paris belonged to Knochen. He was often seen frequenting its numerous salons, leading the life of a society man. Using his culture and wit to impress those who needed to be impressed, Knochen was always in great demand. Popular at meetings and parties given by active collaborationists, he became familiar not just with the lively gossip of Parisian life, but also succeeded in acquiring vital information about prominent statesmen and politicians. More than any other Nazi in Paris he understood clearly the French economy, public opinion and, most useful of all, the leaders of the Opposition and the Resistance.

While political intelligence remained Knochen's true calling, it was an area in which he felt increasingly overwhelmed. Berlin sensed this. As Head of the Central Security Bureau of the Reich, Heydrich had become concerned that Paris would emerge as the weak link in the police chain he was forging in the conquered countries. Knochen was the only senior police officer in all of Hitler's Europe not to have risen from within the ranks of the Gestapo. In fact, he had not received a single day's training in police work of any description. The Gestapo wanted a Gestapo man in Paris, and it had an uncanny knack of getting what it wanted.

In Berlin, Heinrich Müller, Head of the Gestapo, scanned the lists of his best men and decided to appoint SS-Sturmbannführer Kurt Lischka to the Paris post. Müller telephoned Heydrich to inform him of his choice. Within hours Lischka was preparing to leave for the French capital. He had long hoped for a Paris posting.

Kurt Lischka's forte was the Jewish question. He had specialized in this field since 1938 when he took over the Judenreferat IVB (Jewish Affairs) section of the Gestapo. Towards the end of 1938 he was appointed Head of the Reich Centre for Jewish Emigration in Berlin. The deliberate destruction of the synagogues of Paris was well within his purview. In fact Lischka had been personally responsible for arranging details of the *Kristallnacht* pogrom.

Born in Breslau on August 16, 1909, Kurt Lischka was the son of a medium-ranking bank official. Having studied law and political science in Breslau and Berlin, he became active in various district courts, working in the Provincial Court of Appeal in Breslau. Entering the SS on June 1, 1933, he attained the rank of SS Major within five years. His appointment to Paris as Knochen's deputy represented another steady promotion, another rung on the ladder of the SS.

Unlike Knochen, who remained ignorant of police techniques, Lischka considered himself an expert in the arts of interrogation and investigation. But his methods hardly appeared conventional. In a lecture course for police officials, he had once explained a procedure which he commended to the class. For Lischka, beating up prisoners was far too cruel and unsubtle. Nor was it a method which could be relied upon to bring success. Lischka's technique was certainly novel:

> One has to interrogate a political prisoner by using very polite language. If he doesn't confess, he should be given a meal consisting of nothing but salted herring. No drink whatever should be supplied. The following morning the prisoner should be called back for questioning without being offered anything but salted herring for breakfast. While interrogating the obstinate prisoner the police official should have a hearty breakfast in full view of the prisoner and should drink one cup of coffee after the other. Should the prisoner persist in his denials, he should be returned to his cell and refused a drop of water, but should have as his only food more herring. On the second day the same procedure should be followed; then success is virtually assured.

As the Jews of Paris were soon to discover, Lischka had come to Paris armed with substantially more than barrels of herring. On

November 1, 1940 he took up his post in Paris as Knochen's permanent deputy, dividing his time between two offices: a private house in the Avenue Foch, from where he exercised his functions as head of the police force for the whole of France, and 11 rue de Saussaie, from where he would preside over the Paris area. Before long the Paris Gestapo and Kurt Lischka were synonymous, and the entire German police apparatus in France was firmly within his grip. The following list of items ordered by Lischka soon after his arrival in Paris indicates the nature of everyday Gestapo work:

50 coffins to be added to present supply
150 handcuffs requested by the RSHA
[Reich Main Security Office]
thick curtains for vans taking persons to execution
2,000 litres of fuel oil for burning the corpses of the executed in the Père-Lachaise crematorium
refreshments (whisky, wine, snacks) for the execution squads, preferably to be served in their barracks.

Lischka had been sent to Paris to deal with the Jews. On January 20, 1941, he set about his task. A conference had been called on what was now referred to as the 'Final Solution of the Jewish Problem.' It was attended by embassy officials, the military and the Security police, and Lischka was the representative of the SD. The minutes of that meeting were explicit:

SS-Sturmbannführer Lischka pointed out that, insofar as new measures for dealing with the Jews were concerned, the goal was to achieve the solution of the Jewish problem in Europe, according to the directives the Reich had already issued. To this end, it was proposed that a Central Jewish Office be created in France, or in the occupied zone to begin with, that would be responsible for the following:

1. Handling all police matters relating to Jews (census, index cards, surveillance).

2. Economic control (elimination of Jews from economic life, assistance in transferring Jewish business to Aryans).
3. Propaganda (anti-Jewish propaganda among the French).
4. Establishment of an institute of anti-Jewish studies.

A special Jewish division, a precursor of the Central Jewish Office, has already been organised at Paris Police Headquarters. It is advisable to leave the direction of it to the French now, to avoid the French people's reaction against everything of this sort originated by Germans. Germans will restrict themselves to making suggestions.

By now an atmosphere of anti-Semitism pervaded Paris. Previously anti-Jewish imagery had only seeped periodically from beneath the surface of French society. Now, it was on full display. Or so certain sections of the Parisian press would have its readers believe. The newspapers were full of anti-Jewish sentiment, with the paper *Au Pilori* the undisputed leader. The approach was, to say the least, unsophisticated. Typical headlines read: 'The Jewish question must be resolved immediately by the arrest and deportation of all Jews without exception' and 'The Jewish people has placed itself outside the Moral Laws.' The cinema too became a vehicle for anti-Semitism. For when a film entitled *The Jewish Peril* was shown at the César cinema, Lucien Rebatet, holder of the coveted Prix Renaudot for literature, wrote the following review:

Obviously one cannot properly understand the Jew unless one has seen how they live in their large ghettos in Central Europe, around the Carpathian mountains, in Hungary, and especially Rumania and Russia. The first half of this film was shot in the Polish ghettos by members of the Wehrmacht, shortly after the lightning campaign of 1939. It is a masterpiece of documentary reporting, like almost everything these cameramen in uniform record, whether behind the lines or at the front . . . Of the Jews in Europe at this time, 80 per cent are second or at most third-generation descendants of that European Jewry which has

for centuries harboured and cultivated a hate for Christians –
learning in their Talmud and in their rabbinical schools to cheat
and exploit our race and prepare for a hegemony of Israel. The
Jews we come across daily, here in France, have been able to
adopt a light varnish of French custom and behaviour. But
beneath the superficial Western traits, they are aliens, though
shorn of their beards and robes. We must learn from now on
to recognize in them the eternal Jew – the exotic outsider who
will never belong.

Even less subtle was the edition of *Au Pilori* dated March 14,
1941:

Death to the Jew! Death to meanness, to deceit, to Jewish wiles!
Death to the Jewish cause! Death to Jewish usury! Death to all
that is false, ugly, dirty, repulsive, negroid, cross-bred, Jewish!
Death! Death to the Jew! Yes. Repeat it. Death! D.E.A.T.H.
TO THE JEW! For the Jew is not a man. He is a stinking
beast. We defend ourselves against evil, against death – and
therefore against the Jews.

In Germany persecution of the Jews had been going on for at least
eight years; in France things were still only getting underway.
Knochen and Lischka were aware that there was a good deal of
catching up to do if the Reich and the Greater Reich were truly
to become one.

An avalanche of discriminatory measures followed. On August
31, 1941, all radios belonging to Jews were confiscated. And then
their bicycles suffered the same fate. Ordered by the German
authorities to disconnect all telephones in Jewish households,
the Post Office did as instructed. Jews were then forbidden to
use public telephones. Jewish lawyers were no longer allowed
to practise in cases involving French law. The Prefect of Police
made it illegal for Jews to change their address. A German ruling
followed which made it illegal for Jews to leave home between
eight pm and five am.

Restrictions, prohibitions and decrees proliferated; all public places, parks, theatres and certain shops were soon closed to Jews. Jews were allowed to shop, but only during certain hours of the afternoon, when anything worthwhile would long since have disappeared from the shelves. Virtually every week began with the promulgation of a new discriminatory measure. Jews were barred from public swimming pools, restaurants, cafés, cinemas, concerts, music halls, and markets. Fairs, museums, libraries, public exhibitions, historical monuments, sporting events and camp grounds were all likewise forbidden territory. As for the Métro, Jews were obliged to ride only in the last car. Knochen and Lischka had indeed been hard at work.

Before the ink was dry on one promulgation, another had appeared. Then, on May 29, 1942, the most familiar of all Nazi decrees, a law that made it compulsory for Jews to wear a yellow star. Hastily, 5,000 metres of gold-coloured material were ordered from a company called Barbet-Massin, Popelin Limited, at a special price of twenty-one francs per metre. It was estimated that this would yield at least 400,000 stars, certainly enough to get matters underway. Another company, Wauters and Sons, was given permission to work through the night in order to provide the lettering. The François Service organized the provision of stars, but only in exchange for one coupon of clothing ration-cards. The wording could not have taken long to draft:

It is forbidden for Jews from the age of six upwards to appear in public without wearing the yellow star.

Then came the precise terms of this, the Eighth Ordinance:

It is a six pointed star having the dimensions of the palm of a hand and with black edges. It is to be in yellow material and is to carry in black lettering the inscription 'Jew.' It must be worn, from the age of six years old, and be quite visible on the left hand side of the chest, carefully sewn onto the item of clothing.

After almost two years of German occupation, the badge bearing the word 'Juif' had arrived.

Until the star decree, persecution of the Jews had been largely hidden from the French public. Before that, Jews may have been excluded from concerts, cafés, museums and the like, but the majority of discriminatory measures hardly disrupted everyday life. Now the star was there for all to see. On the Sunday following the publication of the Eighth Ordinance, Jewish veterans set out on a slow but dignified stroll, displaying their stars alongside their military decorations. In the Métro, reports circulated that scores of gentiles had given up their seats for Jews. Even some practising Catholics and one priest appeared with the Jewish sign. It soon became quite clear that the French public did not like the star. In fact, the star provoked the first extensive and open resistance to the anti-Jewish persecution in France. One approach was that of ridicule, a kind of black humour inspired by the Nazi obsession with race. In all the major cities of France, German police and counter-espionage agents discovered Jewish sympathizers wearing yellow flowers, yellow handkerchiefs, or bits of papers with ironic inscriptions like 'Goy' or 'Danny,' the name of a Jewish boyfriend. These protests were monitored by overseas broadcasting organizations, the BBC in London reporting that French university students were wearing badges with the inscription 'JUIF' purporting to stand for 'Jeunesse Universitaire Intellectuelle Française.'

Yet newspapers in the capital stoutly defended the new measures. In the *Cri du Peuple*, under the headline 'In the light of the Yellow Star,' the following observations appeared:

One has only to spend a quarter of an hour on a Sunday, strolling between the Madeleine and the Place de la République, in order to convince oneself of the reality of the Jewish peril. The proportion of passers-by marked with a yellow star surpasses anything one might have imagined. Even the dumbest Gaullist cannot help admitting to himself that they are decidedly too many. Last Sunday on a walk between the Porte St Denis and the rue Montmartre, one of our reporters passed 268 people wearing yellow stars on his side of the street alone, and all in the space of ten minutes.

With the Jews now readily identifiable, certain sections of the press became unstoppable. Before long the same newspaper was producing lengthy attacks against the Jews. The following article headlined 'The Jews, a Leisure Class,' is typical:

Groups of young Jewish men and women, aged between 18 and 30, spend hours every morning sauntering along the elegant paths of the Bois de Boulogne. All that these favoured young people do is repeat the words of the latest news broadcast from the BBC and spout criticism of the French government. Others among them prefer to paddle canoes on the lake or on the river Marne. The swimming pools of Paris are choked with arrogant young Jews joking with each other at the tops of their voices; 'My dear, somehow in a swimsuit you seem quite ordinary. You really look much sharper with a yellow star on.' Are we going to tolerate this gang of idlers? There is no shortage of work. Let us put the Jews to work.

There was more to come. An exhibition was to be organized, its title 'Le Juif et la France.' The Palais Berlitz on the Boulevard des Italiens was selected as a suitable venue. Its goal was to persuade the visitor that France, since the Middle Ages, had been the prey of international Jewry. Or as the guides escorting visitors to the exhibition hall would explain: 'An enormous spider hanging over the entrance will have come to your attention. This spider represents Jewry feasting on the blood of our France.' Sexual perverts, destroyers of tradition, criminals, organizers of the 1939 exodus from Paris, speculators, cheats, of mongol stock – the list of the supposed sins of the Jews was endless. Anything could be pegged on; certainly no one in authority would prevent it. On the contrary, it was the occupying authority which was sponsoring the exhibition.

The exhibition was heralded as a great success, with thousands flocking to it, and the Ministry of Education, based in Vichy, circulated a memorandum to all teaching personnel urging them to encourage pupils to visit the site. Financial incentives were provided: for those on group visits the admission charge would be waived. For sixteen weeks the exhibition drew substantial crowds before Vichy decided that the residents of Marseilles, Nice, Cannes, Toulouse and Lyons should not be deprived of this new and exciting spectacle. Legitimized as never before, anti-Semitism had not only emerged – it was the law.

Shortly after the opening of the exhibition in September 1941, SS-Hauptsturmführer Theodor Dannecker arrived in Paris. It was he who was to be the most powerful impetus behind the 'Final Solution' in France. A twenty-seven-year-old Bavarian lawyer from Munich, Dannecker was sent to Paris by Adolf Eichmann's IVB, the branch of the RSHA in Berlin devoted to Jewish matters. With three years' experience behind him in the anti-Jewish bureaucracy of the SS, the young lawyer now headed the corresponding bureau in the Paris RSHA office, known as the Judenreferat. With Dannecker as its leader, the Judenreferat was to be the most active German agency involved in the long-range planning and formulation of Jewish policy in France, constantly prodding Vichy into more active anti-Jewish measures.

Although formally placed under Knochen's administrative and disciplinary command, in reality Dannecker received his orders directly from Eichmann. With Dannecker also installed on the Avenue Foch, the principal persecutors of French Jewry were now in place: Knochen, the intellectual; Lischka, the bully; and now Dannecker, the bigot – three men who together would savage, maul and mutilate the Jews of France beyond recognition.

And yet at no time did Dannecker's anti-Jewish section command more than two dozen recruits – too few to carry out his programme of persecution. But he could always count on the help of the French authorities. In no time Dannecker had created an umbrella organization, the Union Générale des Israélites de France, or UGIF, as it was more popularly known. The UGIF, the French Jewish Union, brought together under one roof sixty-seven ad hoc

Jewish organizations, thus ensuring Dannecker an ease of control. Next he organized the CGQJ – the Commissariat Générale aux Questions Juives – whose task it was to co-ordinate the broader thrust of anti-Jewish policy.

Then he established the Contrôle des Administrations Provisoires, whose mandate was to liaise with the military over the sequestration of Jewish businesses and factories. Over 20,000 Jewish-owned businesses were to be transferred from their rightful owners into the hands of French profiteers. The criterion for confiscation did not present numerous legal obstacles: anything belonging to a Jew would suffice.

Dannecker was quite satisfied with his speedy progress. Occupied France was most obliging. In a report dated February 22, 1941, he noted:

The French inspectors formed and instructed in collaboration with our section for Jewish affairs today constitute an élite body, as well as training cadres for Frenchmen to be drafted in the future to the anti-Jewish police.

With two more organizations the network would be complete. First, Dannecker established the PQJ – the Police aux Questions Juives – in conjunction with Vichy's Ministry of the Interior. The offices of an American-Jewish welfare agency, The Joint, situated in the rue de Téhéran, were pointedly requisitioned for this purpose. Dannecker's final creation was the Institut des Questions Juives, funded by the Gestapo and designed to give the impression that anti-Semitism was spreading throughout the country as the spontaneous reaction of French people themselves.

Although music by Jewish composers was prohibited by law, even the most tightly drafted decree could not prevent Offenbach's *Cancan* from being played in the city's night spots. A theatre named after the legendary Jewish actress, Sarah Bernhardt, was hastily renamed Théâtre de la Cité. Some Parisian shopkeepers, desperate not to be mistaken for Jews, invented slogans to demonstrate that their pedigree was not tainted in any way. One leading optician coined the phrase 'Lissac is not Isaac,' which was hailed as typically French wit. Outside the Café Dupont, in the Latin Quarter, there was a notice which could easily have been imported from Germany: 'Closed to dogs and Jews.' Even works of art which featured Jews were condemned. For the Nazis showed no hesitation in cutting to shreds any Jewish family portrait in the Louvre, and well over 500 other paintings deemed to be racially unsound were burned: art turned into ash.

Dannecker knew very well that he had not been sent to Paris to organize exhibitions or cut up the canvases of Jewish painters. So amid the scores of anti-Jewish promulgations the occasional round-up of Jews also took place. Nothing systematic, just an occasional *rafle*, or round-up. After isolation and Aryanization, there remained only 'arrestation.'

The first round-up of Jews took place on May 14, 1941. Some 4,000 foreign Jews were 'invited,' as the official documentation put it, by the issue of a green ticket to present themselves to the Commissariat of their quarter in order to take part in 'an identity control.' It was a strange sort of control though, because all participants were instructed to bring along a blanket and various other personal effects. Dannecker had decided that the prisons of Beaune-la-Rolande and Pithiviers should now be filled, and these helpless immigrant Jews became their unwitting occupants.

Worry and fear spread through the Jewish community. Questions were many: Why had they been detained? And what was to become of them? Rumours were rife. Word had it that they would soon be released from the 'lodging camps,' as the prisons were officially described.

On August 20, 1941, some three months after this first *rafle*, a sizeable round-up took place in the eleventh *arrondissement*, where many Jewish artisans and workers lived. Now it was not so much a question of invitation, rather of compulsion. For the entire area was sealed off by the municipal police and the Paris guard, although the actual arrests were made by German gendarmes accompanied by inspectors from the Prefecture of Police. The arrested Jews, this time both French and foreign, were sent to a massive unfinished housing complex at Drancy, on the outskirts of Paris. Six days later all Jewish lawyers were arrested. Some forty members of the Paris Bar were taken from their homes to the Louis Lepine hall at the Prefecture, and from there to Drancy.

The net continued to spread from immigrant Jew to French national, to members of the professional Jewish community, until, on December 12, 1941, the most distinguished members of the Jewish community in Paris were rounded up – prominent doctors, academics, scientists and writers – the 'intégrationistes extraordinaires.'

The grim logic of Nazism ground on. Isolation, Aryanization, arrest. What next? The inevitable: deportation. In fact the eagerness of Lischka and Dannecker to deport French Jewry surpassed that of Eichmann himself. Could Berlin not get things moving more speedily? Lischka sent an urgent telegram to Eichmann in February 1942:

> Subject: deportation to the East of Jews and young communists . . . with a view towards reinforcing German authority in the occupied zone, it becomes urgent to deport as rapidly as possible the thousand Jews arrested during the action of December 12, 1941. In addition to the fact that our service and the Commandant of Greater Paris have been burdened with an avalanche of requests for the liberation of these Jews, one must note that the fact that they have not been deported to date is interpreted on the French side as weakness. I am requesting the adoption of a special procedure in this individual case. Please notify by telegram.

A week later, on March 1, Eichmann replied affirmatively to Knochen:

> One thousand Jews will immediately be taken into custody after the discussions currently underway on the timetable, and will be taken to a reception camp in the Reich. Since SS-Hauptsturmführer Dannecker, Rapportführer for Jewish Affairs

action will be discussed
942 . . .

volition, but on Lischka's
ceived the green light from
bearing the good news. The
tation of Jews. A pretext was
as by way of reprisal for Jewish
e. After almost three months of
rat had finally succeeded in obtain-

oy was Dannecker himself. One thou-
lve Jews left Drancy for an unknown
, 1942. They set off in third-class car-
es to escape the ordeal of freight cars.
self arrested in the round-up of December
story of this first convoy's departure from

g high. People
of what the
restrictions
o. Travelling
experience,
suburban
hrough the
ways filled
obliged to
th yellow
t worry
At least
iculars
ty was
re so.
mon
the
uld
. It
the
on

city to the railroad station under the watch
he townspeople who look on silently, sombrely,
, but discreetly showing their encouragement and
by their gestures. The especially thin silhouettes of
eportees, their earth-coloured faces, and unsteady walk
ced a shattering effect on the crowd. No one is yet
stomed to such spectacles. Near the station there is a
owd, and miraculously one recognises women who have come
rom Paris, warned of the departure no one knows how. The
Germans prevent them from coming close to the ranks and the
last goodbye is said at a distance . . . At the station one waits
for the train which must come from Paris, bringing 550 other
deportees taken the same day from Drancy. It arrives soon and
when it begins to move it is the first of 200 trains of deportees
which will travel towards Germany. This one will take away
1,100 men with their thoughts, their sufferings, their tenderness
and their hatreds.

47

In the Jewish quarters of Paris, tension was runni
were living precariously from day to day, unsur
future would bring. Yet somehow, despite the da
and arrests, ordinary activities continued. They had
home after work was a particularly uncomfortabl
beginning with a stampede by commuters for the fe
trains still running. The Métro was erratic, speeding
many stations which had been shut down. Trains were a
to capacity, especially in the last car where the Jews were
ride. There they were, poor Jews, rich Jews, bedecked w
stars, attempting to go about their daily lives. Most did n
unduly about Drancy, or indeed that first deportation.
not outwardly. In fact, few people knew the precise pa
of deportation, of who was going where and why. The c
always full of rumour, whispers and gossip. Now all the m

That first deportation from Paris had a good deal in co
with the First Ordinance, in that it was by definition onl
beginning of a process. Of course, most Jews could not, or w
not, see it. As the spring of 1942 drew on, the rumours persiste
was said that mass round-ups were going to take place. But in
Paris of Knochen, Lischka and Dannecker, the Jewish populati
had little idea of who or what to believe.

4

Paulette

Paulette Szlifke knew what to believe. And who to believe. There could be no question of deluding Paulette. Unlike many of her contemporaries, she harboured no illusions about the nature of the occupying regime. Although only sixteen, Paulette knew precisely where she stood on each of the principal issues of the day, from Nazi promulgation to national collaboration. For Paulette to have conducted herself otherwise was unthinkable, if not contemptible. Her world was far removed from the sophistication of the Kohn family, in which Philippe was sheltered from the everyday realities of National Socialism. For while Philippe Kohn remained closeted by his parents, Paulette Szlifke had been out on the streets, receiving an education of an altogether more radical nature.

From the day the Germans had invaded France, young Paulette Szlifke had been obliged to make an enormous leap of development, propelling herself from childhood into womanhood and bypassing her adolescence.

When Paulette was handed her yellow star, her standard-edition 'JUIF,' it had prompted a bitter battle in the Szlifke household. Unlike many youngsters who wore the star with apparent ease, Paulette was insulted by the very fact of its issue. Deeming it no different from the branding of a beast and ignoring the pleas of her mother Yentyl, she knew that she would be unable to wear hers for long. Barely forty-eight hours after her mother's meticulous stitches had been completed, Paulette's star was tucked away in a drawer at home. Aware that the significance of the Eighth Ordinance was considerably more than a German preoccupation with orderliness and efficiency, Paulette resolved to have nothing to do with it.

Yentyl Szlifke could not understand her daughter's refusal to comply with the law and took to complaining endlessly to friends, and to anyone else who would listen, that teenagers appeared no longer to respect authority. Only some weeks later did Yentyl Szlifke realize what should have been obvious much earlier: wearing the star automatically disqualified her daughter from going to the cinema, one of her favourite pastimes. Yentyl rebuked herself for not having made the connection sooner. In fact, she was by no means averse to the occasional film herself.

Paulette's mother could not have been further from the mark. For if Paulette wanted to see a film, she did so with a particular purpose, having nothing to do with an interest in the arts. For Paulette Szlifke, seeing a film now meant conducting business of an altogether different kind. She would always take a balcony seat, from which she would launch into the darkened air a patriotic message of defiance. The leaflets contained a plea to the people to join in the struggle; they told the truth about the round-ups, the deportations and the executions. And then Paulette would hastily leave, seeking safer ground. It took some time for her heart to return to its normal beat. Obviously it was inadvisable to brandish a yellow star announcing one's identity to friend and foe alike, when engaging in such activities.

Only sixteen, but already shrewd. Who could be trusted? It was best to leave nothing to chance. While in or near her *arrondissement,* she would carry books and bags close to her chest so that neighbours and friends would assume that she, like thousands of others, bore that dark and distinctive Gothic lettering 'JUIF.' Despite protracted disagreements with her parents about the star, Paulette remained a devoted daughter. She went to great lengths not to involve them in any way, keeping them entirely ignorant of her new and clandestine activities.

Paulette was greatly assisted by the fact that she looked completely Aryan with her striking fair hair and deep blue eyes. Her petite frame and figure gave the appearance of a rather fragile and vulnerable young girl. It was the perfect front, one which she would increasingly use to her advantage.

Paulette's radicalism was attributable largely to her father, Efrayim Szlifke, who was born in a small Polish 'shteitel' shortly before the turn of the century. Outraged by working conditions in his homeland, he became an outspoken trade union activist. His consistent campaigning on behalf of the working class had once led to his imprisonment, about which Paulette had often boasted to her friends. In fact, this was precisely why he had fled Poland in the first place: the desire to leave repression behind once and for all. Settled in France, he soon learned that much remained to be done, despite his host country's historic commitment to the concept of universal liberty, equality and fraternity. Once again he launched himself into the familiar world of the labour movement. Paris and Poland could hardly have seemed further apart, but for Efrayim Szlifke the principle of fighting exploitation transcended national boundaries. It was in this atmosphere of radicalism that Paulette had grown up.

The Szlifkes were not a religious family, at least not in the sense of observing every custom and High Holy Day. Like the Kohns, they had abandoned the traditional Friday-night meal; only Passover merited any visible sign of religious observance. There was simply not enough time for the rigours of religion and ritual. The characteristics shared by the Kohn and Szlifke households ceased at this point. For while the Kohn family had ensconced itself in the French way of life for several generations, the Szlifkes remained profoundly Jewish, new immigrants from the East proudly clinging to their roots and traditions.

In the Szlifke household Yiddish remained the principal language. In the years between the two world wars, well over a hundred Yiddish periodicals were established to serve and inform the community. Before the arrival of the Germans, there existed in Paris a network of some ten Yiddish supplementary schools run under communist auspices and established to provide a class-conscious Jewish education. The objective was to draw the children of workers away from the religious chauvinist schools run by the Jewish bourgeoisie. Paulette Szlifke was thus brought up immersed in a wealth of Jewish tradition, singing Jewish songs handed down from one generation to the next, listening with fascination to exciting tales drawn from Jewish folklore. Paulette was certainly not known for her religious adherence, but her every move was imbued with the essence of Judaism.

While the Kohn family continued to live in isolation from these new and energetic immigrant communities, Paulette had grown up alongside scores of German Jews who had fled either from Hitler's Germany or from the pogroms and oppression of the East. Time and again she had listened with a mixture of horror and fascination to the details of *Kristallnacht*. For Paulette there was really only one lesson: the Jews had to learn to fight for themselves.

The Szlifkes lived in a run-down apartment at 14 rue de Vaucouleurs on the third floor of the block. Paulette's father ran a small furrier's workshop a little further down the road at number 34. The street was in Belleville, one of the areas where these newly arrived working-class Jews had concentrated. It was the heart of the ghetto. Efrayim Szlifke worked long hours in his workshop, stretching and tacking down sheepskins, his teeth holding an array of tacks, the tiny furrier's hammer rhythmically beating away in his hand.

The Kohns lived in the sixteenth *arrondissement*; the Szlifkes in the eleventh. Numerically, they were separated by just five *arrondissements*. But those five *arrondissements* were separated by some five centuries of change. For whereas the Kohns took for granted their place in Europe's smartest city, the Szlifkes' world was one of kosher butchers, Jewish bakeries and booksellers displaying their wares in large Hebrew script. On Saturdays scores of bearded men would appear, immaculate in their traditional black caftans, their clothes blending naturally into the narrow streets; tailors, pressers, printers and pleaters all around.

The Szlifkes' flat was typical of the district. There was a constant smell of dampness and pollution. They had neither bathroom nor running water, and there was just one toilet between two floors, which all the occupants shared. Efrayim Szlifke remained convinced that the only hope for material improvement and uplift lay in the Jewish labour movement.

Life in occupied Paris was not always so grim, though, even for the Jews. On warm summer evenings, people would linger on their terraces sipping synthetic aperitifs and admiring the view of the city. Paris looked beautiful in the early evening light, its streets bare of cars because of the shortage of petrol, with only the occasional bicycle quietly passing by. For Paulette, there remained one overriding blemish: the presence of countless white billboards edged in black and with stark German lettering.

Every morning Efrayim Szlifke would rise early and set off for his workshop. It was barely a minute's walk from his home. To make any money, particularly in the fur trade, Efrayim had to be up at the crack of dawn. Never one to shy away from hard work, Paulette's father had been cutting and sewing for as long as he could remember. Before arriving at the workshop, Efrayim Szlifke would first buy his morning paper, the Yiddish daily *Nayer Presser*, from a cheerful woman who ran the small *tabac*. Hers was one of the handful of non-Jewish shops in the entire neighbourhood. One morning, though, she made it clear that there was other, more urgent, business to discuss.

It was August 21, 1941. The *tabac* lady had somehow learned there was to be a *rafle* of all Jewish men in the eleventh *arrondissement*. Taking her regular customer to one side, she whispered that he would be wise to absent himself from the area for at least that day. Efrayim Szlifke, grateful for her advice, hurried to his workshop. Once inside, he locked the door behind him. Never had he been happier to see the familiar sight of his tatty old machinery.

The lady had been right. A round-up was scheduled to take place, and Efrayim was on the list. When the Germans knocked on the door for him, Paulette's mother quietly explained that he was away. It was hardly a credible story, but it seemed to satisfy the questioners. Queries could always be dealt with later. Orders had been issued stating simply that Jews who were at home were to be detained. Those arrested were immediately dispatched to Drancy, now the major detention centre for the Jews of Paris. At Drancy some were apparently speaking of a journey to the East. For the Szlifkes, however, the panic was over.

Another *rafle*. Nothing extraordinary about that. Some had been taken; others were lucky or cunning enough to have dodged the latest haul. And then the return to apparent normality. At least this was the case for Efrayim Szlifke. His priority was simple: to return to work without further delay. For Paulette, however, her father's near-arrest was a watershed. For if previously she merely had been dabbling in the Resistance – a leaflet here, a tract there – now she launched herself into the movement.

Resistance to the Germans took a number of forms. For example, while French postal workers had welcomed the Germans sourly, they soon found themselves providing long-distance telephone facilities. It was part of Vichy's plan of submissive collaboration. Two large cables were to be laid from Paris: one via Metz, the other via Strasbourg. Ultimately both would extend to the German defence headquarters. With the cables under particularly heavy guard, virtually every French operator had an armed German close by. The security implications were obvious. Nonetheless, from the autumn of 1940 on, a small group of linesmen operating within the Resistance had been working on the problem of interception. By April 1942, with a combination of technical skill and sheer luck, they had succeeded in tapping the Paris-Metz cable at Noisy-le-Grand, near Paris. They recorded every word uttered until December of that year. However, a fortnight after they had succeeded in tapping the other cable as well, they were caught in the act of interception. Almost all were killed, but not before they had passed on by wireless to London a vast amount of important material.

The resistance of Paulette Szlifke was somewhat more modest. Her conviction was simple and straightforward: that something was better than nothing. Sharing the objectives of the linesmen and inspired by their daring, Paulette saw an opportunity to strike. Now working full-time in the Resistance, she had managed to obtain forged identity papers. Using the official stamp of her former high school, she forged a *carte d'identité scolaire*, presenting herself to the world at large and to prospective employers in particular as a mere schoolgirl, of Aryan stock of course. To any hostile inquirer, the name was Marie-Thérèse Muldaise, a Brittany girl born and bred.

Paulette applied for a job in a small furrier's workshop, a company very much involved in the war effort. Among other things the factory produced gloves for German soldiers on the bitterly cold eastern front. All factory workers had been issued a special pass, since production had been deemed important to the German war effort. Paulette Szlifke was hired as a machine-hand, able to convince her employers that she knew how to thread and operate a machine. Working in collaboration with another colleague in the Resistance, she managed on several occasions to bring the entire factory to a halt.

Industrial sabotage was, in fact, a relatively simple affair. Since the electrical meters and fuses were situated in a corridor well away from the factory floor, the panels were easily accessible. Fortunately, too, the factory management had not thought to post a guard there. It was hardly the work of a skilled technician: all Paulette had to do was pull at a few fuses to bring work to a standstill. It worked, much to her delight, several times. The greater her success within the factory, the more courageous she became. But soon it became clear that she must change tactics before she got caught.

Hundreds of animal skins were stacked in a concealed corner of the factory waiting to become fur-lined gloves. It was too good an opportunity to miss. One match did the trick. Within minutes all the skins had been destroyed. The last person in the factory to be suspected was the small, innocent-looking sixteen-year-old, Marie-Thérèse Muldaise. Paulette Szlifke quietly moved on from her machining job. There was now other work to be done.

Occasionally Paulette would ride in the last Métro car, disguising the absence of her yellow star. Whenever in the vicinity of the eleventh *arrondissement*, however, she would always show extreme caution, aware that not all neighbours were as friendly as their smiles might suggest. On returning home one evening, she found herself just two stops from Couronnes, the station nearest the rue de Vaucouleurs. It was almost eight o'clock. In one hour the curfew ordered by the Military Governor of 'Gross Paris' would lock the city for another night. There was plenty of time really, but since the arrival of the Germans the atmosphere of the Métro had changed beyond recognition. Suddenly, her heart froze. All passengers were being made to pass through an identity control, with dozens of French police massed behind a barrier by the exit. A stern voice barked out the inevitable message: 'Vos papiers. Vos papiers, s'il vous plaît.'

Hastily, Paulette made the transition from Jewish rebel into the law-abiding Catholic schoolgirl, Marie-Thérèse. It was by no means an easy change, with scores of trained eyes peering down upon her, waiting for the first nerve to break. Would the falsified stamp of her high school now survive its first rigorous inspection? Although trembling within, to the outside world, and in particular to the enormous policeman inspecting her papers, Marie-Thérèse appeared to present not even the remotest cause for concern.

'Bonsoir Madamemoiselle. Et merci.'

Paulette smiled thinly at the policeman and walked towards the familiar territory of the dreary and dilapidated rue de Vaucouleurs. The old ghetto had never looked more enticing.

*   *   *

The Avenue Foch offices of the Gestapo were swarming with activity. Hauptsturmführer Theodor Dannecker was totally absorbed in his work. He loved the fast pace. He was confident that he would make a success of his Paris posting; not once had the quality of his work been called into question by his superiors. For some weeks Dannecker had been preoccupied with the organization of something rather obscure. It was known to only a handful of senior Nazis that he was responsible for the fine print of operation 'Spring Wind.' The French Ministry of the Interior likewise was working at full speed. Everyone appeared to be bracing themselves for the operation as if preparing for a major offensive in battle.

Dannecker had to chair a final meeting with the French authorities before things could really get underway. The officials assembled in his large office. Every detail appeared to have been considered: transportation, timetables, capacities and camps. 'Spring Wind' was in fact the code name for a major round-up. Dannecker revealed that the purpose of this operation was to round up, detain and then deport no fewer than 28,000 Jews. Never before had such figures been contemplated.

The *rafle* was originally planned for the night of July 13–14. However, since that was the eve of Bastille Day, when people would be out on the streets, wearing tricolor costumes, the mood of nationalism could easily turn ugly. Aware that nothing could be left to chance, Dannecker reluctantly agreed for 'Spring Wind' to be delayed until the celebrations were over.

Once again the city was rife with rumour. Word had it that something major was about to break. On the eve of operation 'Spring Wind,' Paulette slept over with a friend, not returning to the rue de Vaucouleurs. She had been out on another 'action'; this time the burning of some German signposts in the twentieth *arrondissement*. It had been successful, but seldom was an 'action' accomplished without its share of fear and trembling. It was another of her acts of sabotage, the frequency and audacity of which were increasing almost daily.

'Spring Wind' had been re-scheduled for July 16–17. Armand Kohn was working late at the Rothschild Hospital. As Chief Administrator, he had a few pressing problems. The Rothschild was not exactly a prison, but neither was it an ordinary hospital; rather it was an anomalous hybrid of the two. Certainly people came to be cured of illness, but they were by no means free to come and go as they pleased. The barbed wire circling the hospital made that only too clear. The main problem on Armand Kohn's mind was the fact that there appeared to be certain people on the hospital staff who were bent on causing trouble. People were coming and going more readily than should have been the case. Kohn suspected that members of the Resistance were working within the hospital. But, surrounded by established doctors and eminent Jewish surgeons, he was quite unable to attribute blame with any degree of precision.

Resistance! The word cut no ice with Kohn. Anyone could break the rules. Despising those who elected to live in the murky world of illegality, he even went so far as to consider that *he* represented the true spirit of resistance: doing what he could every now and then to admit to the hospital various people who approached him. A word in his ear had resulted in the sudden appearance of a hospital bed on more than one occasion. With a combination of sophistication and subtlety, Armand Kohn was doing what he could to help. Anyone could be out on the streets, bombing this and blasting that.

Kohn knew that if the irregularities at the hospital were to continue, then he would be obliged to make the hospital regime still more authoritarian. He had in mind to draw up certain restrictive directives, but on the eve of 'Operation Spring Wind,' he decided to do so only if matters deteriorated further. Relieved at finally having made a decision, he called for his driver to take him back to the healthier environs of the sixteenth *arrondissement*.

Armand Kohn had certainly heard the whispered rumours now circulating in the city. 'Operation Spring Wind' had become the worst-kept secret in the whole of Paris. All this talk of a large round-up. Kohn did not believe a word of it. And the reason was very simple: the information did not fit into his preconceived ideas about the occupying regime.

In fact, young Paulette, who had just turned seventeen, was more in touch with the reality of the German occupation than the cautious Armand Kohn. The Rothschild chief consistently refused to digest unpalatable information. Perhaps the reality of 'Operation Spring Wind' would compel him to be less inflexible. Or were these incessant whispers merely part of another campaign designed to make the Jews of Paris, rich and poor alike, feel even less secure?

Paulette Szlifke and Armand Kohn had only one thing in common: neither had any idea of the magnitude of Theodor Dannecker's master plan. 'Spring Wind' sounded rather mild. The truth was, a powerful tornado was poised to strike.

5

La Grande Rafle

Theodor Dannecker may have masterminded the operation, but 'Vent Printanier,' as it was known in French, was to be a specifically French undertaking. Every city official seemed to be involved in its execution. The gendarmerie, the mobile guard, the judiciary police, bailiffs, detectives and patrolmen – all were assembled and waiting to strike. The city's media and public transport facilities were also ready to swing into action. No fewer than 888 arrest teams of three or four men each were in the process of receiving their final briefings. Mistakes would not be tolerated. In all, more than 9,000 men were waiting for zero hour.

At the academy of police training, lectures were cancelled for the day. Student police officers were themselves to participate in the round-ups, their instructors having realized that this was a practical exercise worth any number of classroom hours. The detailed instructions indicated how harsh the operation would be:

1. As soon as the identity of a listed Jew has been confirmed, inspectors and guards are to proceed with the arrest, taking no notice of any protest or argument the prisoner may offer.
2. Every Jew listed is to be brought to the preliminary collecting centre, no notice being taken of the state of health of the prisoners or exceptions made for that reason.

And where were the 27,388 prospective prisoners? For the most part in bed. With the streets of Paris empty and shutters firmly closed for the night, zero hour had quietly arrived.

At four in the morning squads of French police burst into the homes of Jews all over Paris. Discovering their whereabouts had presented few practical problems, for in accordance with the requirements of the First Ordinance, most Jews had long ago registered with the police.

The pattern soon became familiar. First, the area would be sealed off. Then the arrest teams, with their long lists, would enter the buildings and knock on the door of the family they sought. Thousands of apartment blocks were swarming with police. In some buildings, so many families were listed that a single arrest team was quite unable to cope, and several teams were to be seen working at one address, hurrying up and down shabby staircases, calling out surnames that they could barely pronounce. Like some pitiless tide, these uniformed teams would overrun a building, working their way from floor to floor, furiously banging on doors and shouting, 'Police . . . Open up . . . Police . . . Open up.'

As Paris awoke on the morning of Thursday July 16, 1942, people were struck by the sight of Jewish family groups walking in silence, the father and mother carrying bundles and packages, holding their children by the hand. Men on their way to work, concierges awakened by the noise, shopkeepers opening their stores – these early-to-rise Parisians could not believe the spectacle before them.

Initially many Jews were reassured by the French uniformed officers who greeted them. At least there was no sign of the Germans. Hearing instructions issued in French, and seeing the eminently proper procedures followed by the arresting officers, some Jews felt they were in safe hands. The French police went about the arrests with a complacent calm, and in simple terms of policing their behaviour could not be criticized.

The months of meticulous planning appeared to have foreseen every eventuality. Gas and electricity were to be turned off, animals left with the concierge. Arresting officers were instructed to fill out a card giving the relevant information concerning each arrest, including the name of the person in whose care the apartment keys had been left.

Whenever a door remained shut after the policeman's knock, the chances were that a family had escaped. Some policemen did not seek to disguise their relief. All they had to do now was to note that no one was at home. The guidelines had been quite explicit: 'Where an individual named on the list has not been arrested, guards and inspectors are to give the reasons for the failure, keeping their report brief and to the point.' Other policemen were rather more enthusiastic in the execution of their duty, one going so far as to note in his report, 'If only we had the necessary authorization, we would ferret out these Jews who think they can dump themselves on us.' Many were so conscientious that they forced their way into apartments – strictly against instructions.

The rules had been quite explicit. Arrests were to be carried out without regard to the state of health. And so they were. Women on the point of giving birth, children with measles, scarlet fever, chicken pox, whooping cough and mumps; all were detained.

Had Dannecker's guidelines been drafted as comprehensively as possible? Evidently not. For they had not dealt with the possibility that a person listed for arrest might have just passed away. There were at least three such cases that day, one of which was a newborn baby. Here was an opportunity for improvisation, for police initiative at its best. The officers wrapped the dead in blankets and the corpses were carried off to the collecting centres, along with all the other detainees.

During the course of *La Grande Rafle*, over one hundred people decided to commit suicide, and twenty-four died from sickness, two of whom were women in the full throes of childbirth. It was a *rafle* conducted in keeping with the best of French traditions, for at noon the policemen returned to their posts to have lunch while the higher-ranked and better paid set off to nearby restaurants. Only after the sacred *déjeuner* could the manhunt continue. From late morning until late afternoon, the next shift of policemen returned to those apartments found empty earlier in the day. The streets were thoroughly combed and many Jews, afraid to return home and wandering about aimlessly, were arrested not far from their homes.

News of the arrests spread quickly through the city, but many Parisians witnessed horrific scenes: women fainting and children wailing as they sensed their parents' despair. One mother threw her four children out of the window of her fifth-floor apartment as the door was being forced, then leapt after them. A ten-year-old girl, crazed with fear, jumped from the sixth floor. The police broke into another apartment to find a man with his mouth over the gas outlet, half-asphyxiated. In Montreuil a doctor killed himself and his entire family with hypodermic injections.

The machinery of operation 'Spring Wind' now had a momentum of its own. Fifty buses had been requisitioned from the *Compagnie des Transports*. These Renault buses, with their central aisles, and leather-upholstered seats in the first-class section, now set off on a series of journeys, laden with passengers become prisoners. It was to be a shuttle service between the collecting centres in the city and the *Vélodrome d'Hiver*, where families with children were to be kept, and the detention centre of Drancy which had been prepared for those adults without children. The *Vél d'Hiv*, as Parisians knew it, was a large indoor sports stadium in the fifteenth *arrondissement*. It had already hosted many political rallies, including anti-Semitic demonstrations.

Outside the stadium, the rue Nelaton looked like a bus terminal. Hundreds of buses jammed with people were busily coming and going. Once deposited on the pavement outside the gates, the Jews stood in a daze, with children and bundles cluttered around them. Moments later these Jewish families were shepherded through the arena's swinging doors. Soon the entire ground-floor arena was filled. With buses continuing to arrive every ten minutes or so, newcomers found themselves forced onto the tiers above. Altogether 7,000 Jews were to be interned there, of whom just over 4,000 were children.

The first day at the *Vél d'Hiv* was one of complete chaos. No food was provided. People had been instructed to bring their own provisions for two days, but there was not a drop of water and no milk for the children. In no time at all the air had become unbreathable, stinking, and thick with dust. Eyes smarted and throats were parched. The earlier restraint shown by the French police began to crumble, the eighty armed guards there showing no signs of relenting.

Some detainees became hysterical. One father, about forty years old, just sat hugging his knees, hands limp, his face completely without expression. His Polish wife wrung her hands and moaned, while their daughter, a child no more than eight years old, hung on to her mother, trying to kiss her while whispering words of comfort in French. Another woman, either because she had gone out of her mind or because she had decided to take her own life, threw herself to the ground and, leaning on her arms, banged her head on the cement floor. Bystanders watched helplessly until she was overpowered and taken to the centre of the arena. A medical report noted that: 'We had to tie down the insane men and women to stretchers and hide them from the rest of the crowd. Our orders were to treat them as shams.'

One woman slashed her wrists with the splinters of a broken mirror. By the time someone noticed, she had fainted from loss of blood. In all there were some thirty suicide attempts, ten successful. Most of the suicides threw themselves from the highest tier of the arena. As they landed with a dull thud on the track below, the crowd would back away, screaming. These unfortunates were then picked up, wounded, gasping, dying or dead.

The toilets – just ten for 7,000 people – had become so blocked that they were virtually unusable. For five days the detainees went without food or water. Babies were born. Some people died. Others went insane. Everyone was filthy.

On the evening of July 16, André Baur, the Secretary-General of the Union Générale des Israélites en France, was allowed to enter the *Vél d'Hiv*. The following is his account of what he saw:

The entire enclosure was crawling with activity. We arrived at the central stage by the tunnel. An enormous crowd in the galleries, where all the seats appeared to be taken. From time to time, young people brought bowls of water and everyone hurried to fill their bottles, pots or jam jars. On the stage, on the right after coming out of the tunnel, stretchers are lying on which women and children moan. In a small enclosure on the left, the Red Cross has installed an ambulance. Two doctors and nurses are busy at work. One gets the impression that there are only children and sick people. The nurses have tears in their eyes, the policemen are heartsick. There is no trace of even the slightest organisation, no direction, no chief or too many of them . . .

There was, in addition, the summer's heat with which to contend, followed by the onset of cold nights. Before long, hundreds of people were suffering from chronic diarrhoea and dysentery, and a terrible odour soon infested the entire arena. As the long hours stretched into days a sense of abandonment set in. It was a most remarkable spectacle: thousands of people penned in like cattle in this, the most civilized city in the world.

By one o'clock in the afternoon of Friday July 17, operation 'Spring Wind' had finally came to an end. The overworked buses were dispatched to resume normal service. The siege on the quarters with the heaviest Jewish populations was lifted. Inside the *Vél d'Hiv*, however, the suffering continued. The ruling was, from both French and German quarters, that only two Jewish doctors could be on duty there at any one time. The UGIF organized a rota system of ten volunteer doctors. In the centre of the arena a makeshift first-aid post was set up, where doctors and nurses worked with great dedication, despite their limited supplies. Inside the stadium the most commonly prescribed medication was aspirin. Aspirin for heart attacks, aspirin for kidney failure, aspirin for broken limbs, aspirin for miscarriage. In the circumstances, there was little else that could be done.

News of *La Grande Rafle* continued to spread throughout the city. In cafés, shops and offices, it was the sole topic of conversation. Only one question could be answered with any degree of certainty: the whereabouts of those who had been arrested. Everyone knew what was going on at the *Vélodrome d'Hiver*. Some people had actually gone there and reported on the sports-arena-turned-prison, the commotion from which could be clearly heard in the adjoining streets.

At night the gates were closed, shutting in the stench, which of all the physical discomforts proved the most difficult to bear. Once the arena was closed for the night, not one opening or ventilation shaft was in operation. As the lavatories ceased to function, urine began to trickle down from the upper tiers, where people had been obliged to relieve themselves.

*   *   *

Paulette Szlifke always liked to think that she was one step ahead. Through her contacts in the clandestine organization Solidarité, she had learned that a big round-up was to take place. Virtually everyone had heard the rumour. Even so, her parents would have to be warned. She decided to be up bright and early that Thursday morning. By the time of her arrival at the rue de Vaucouleurs, however, the round-ups were in full swing. Not only that, the rue de Vaucouleurs had been sealed off. The neighbourhood was swarming with police.

Paulette approached her parents' apartment, trying to convince herself that there was little to fear. As young Marie-Thérèse Muldaise she had nothing to hide. This technique of self-deception was never entirely successful, but Paulette clung to it nonetheless. Her father was at his workshop just a few doors away. Yentyl was preparing a knapsack when Paulette arrived.

For once in her life Yentyl Szlifke did not argue. Now their roles were reversed: Paulette instructed her mother to join her father at the workshop. The plan was simple: Yentyl was to make a dash for it, and hope that she would not be caught. As she scuttled off to number 34, she remained preoccupied, frustrated at not having finished her ironing, and at having left the knapsack in the apartment.

For the greater part of the day of *La Grande Rafle*, Paulette Szlifke walked through the streets of Paris, dodging a police cordon here, cutting through a backstreet there. Solidarité had provided her with the address of a safe-house in Clamart. Heading towards the Porte de Versailles, she took a bus to her secret rendezvous.

The month of July 1942 was not a good one for Solidarité, for the Germans were taking increasingly firm action against the Resistance. A week before *La Grande Rafle*, a warning had appeared throughout Paris. It described what measures would be taken against the family of anyone so bold as to oppose the might of the Reich:

1. All the male next of kin in the ascending line, as well as brothers-in-law and cousins over eighteen years of age, will be shot.
2. All female next of kin similarly related will be condemned.
3. All children of men and women against whom these measures are taken, up to the age of seventeen years, will be put into a house of correction controlled by the German authorities.

As for resisting *La Grande Rafle*, there was little to be done. All Solidarité could manage was for two social workers to go to the stadium to report on the situation. In addition, two other women were dispatched to the rue Nelaton. They were the wives of prisoners of war and protected for that reason, theoretically at least. These women would approach the stadium gates as often as twenty times a day, loaded up with baskets of food, in the hope that the guards would let them in. Sometimes they did, sometimes they did not.

Paulette Szlifke was well aware of the risks she ran daily. Two days after *La Grande Rafle*, she returned to her family's apartment in the rue de Vaucouleurs. The neighbourhood seemed deserted. A seal had not yet been applied to the front door of their flat, unlike many other apartments in their block. Gathering an assortment of clothes, bed-covers, pots and pans, Paulette took them to her parents who had been sleeping on the floor of the workshop. They had been living in a state of permanent anguish. The last forty-eight hours had been one prolonged nightmare. Efrayim Szlifke had had enough. He was no longer able to bear the confines of his workshop, where cloth, material and skins were crammed into every available space. That workshop had been designed to confer freedom on the Szlifkes, yet now it served as their prison.

The resistance movement in Paris was the source of all information. Certainly it gave Paulette her view of the world. Solidarité had been able to provide her with a *chambre de bonne* in the twentieth *arrondissement*. The lift went up to the fifth floor, from where there was a walk to the tiny garret above. At least here she would be safe. From that solitary room she would travel back every other day to visit her parents and take them whatever food she had managed to obtain. Knowing when and where to shop in occupied Paris was itself a highly skilled business. Efrayim Szlifke was especially grateful for the cigarette ends which Paulette would faithfully gather for him. A confirmed chain-smoker, he relied on these to steer him through the long and lonely days.

*   *   *

Some Jews had chosen the opposite of Paulette's path, electing to live in the world of legality, as pronounced upon and decreed by the Reich or Vichy. Foremost among such Jews was the organization UGIF. Its members had staked all on reaching some sort of a compromise with the Germans. At the time of *La Grande Rafle* they found themselves faced with the acute problem of what constituted an honourable course of action. At what point did cautious co-operation become active collaboration? On the eve of the big round-up, for example, UGIF had employed women to make labels for prospective deportees. Could such acts be justified? As for the round-ups themselves, the UGIF line was apparently straightforward, at least superficially. Being entirely powerless to prevent the arrests, UGIF would limit itself to the provision of medical aid. That the role of UGIF was becoming increasingly ambiguous was graphically demonstrated when André Baur visited the *Vélodrome d'Hiver* with a view to compiling a report. As soon as he set foot inside the stadium he received the sort of reception a leader of the Jewish community would hardly have expected, for he was booed and insulted. Every adult Jew incarcerated there knew that any Jew bearing the beige or yellow UGIF card had been exempt from arrest. For Baur, this brief visit to the *Vél d'Hiv* was the beginning of the painful realization that the role of UGIF was fatally flawed, for the simple reason that there could be no compromise with the Germans.

Another prominent member of the UGIF was Armand Kohn. Unlike Baur, Kohn had yet to reach any such painful conclusion. Despite the excesses of *La Grande Rafle*, and the incarceration of 7,000 souls, Armand Kohn remained convinced that his policy of rigorous adherence to the law was correct. Certainly the chief administrator of the Rothschild Hospital was treading an extremely delicate path. It was not as if the brutality of *La Grande Rafle* had bypassed the territory over which he presided. Quite the contrary.

The hospital had actually been cleared in preparation for the round-up, just as the Beaune-la-Rolande and Pithiviers camps had been emptied to make way for the Jews about to be arrested. At six o'clock on the morning of July 3, the hospital had been surrounded by both uniformed and plain-clothed police, while the administrative staff, under Armand Kohn, were informed that all patients who had originally come from Drancy had to be handed over. This was not a matter for deliberation; it was an ultimatum. Armand Kohn had no choice but to agree.

The hospital was cleared briskly, the police ignoring the protests of the sick. Only those so ill as to be on the verge of coma were permitted the luxury of a stretcher. Lacking proper clothing, they were whisked off in nightshirts and pyjamas. Some were driven away in police vans, handcuffed to one another. It took a little over an hour before the hospital was cleared. The Rothschild had become the most extraordinary hospital in the land. For unlike in other medical institutions, it never was the intention that patients treated there should return home fit and healthy, able to resume a normal life.

All of this in Paris? This, and more. The arrest of adults was one thing; the arrest of children quite another. Altogether 4,051 children were seized in *La Grande Rafle*. The rue des Écouffes was a tragic sight that Thursday. At number 22 alone, over forty policemen were required. There were so many children in the building it looked like a kindergarten. There were the Goldzimmers with three children, the Najmanns with their three, the Sacanis with five, the Schlomenes with another three, and Mr Wolfowski with his daughter. The bus that took them away made it seem more like a school outing, the children looking out of the windows with the sun beating down on their faces, fists and noses flattened against the glass. Even on this most unusual journey, the little ones had not hesitated to take their customary window seats.

Once inside the *Vélodrome d'Hiver*, children could be seen running about in the centre of the arena, teasing the guards, whose orders were to chase them back to the tiers. For many, the contrast between children playing happily on the track and parents in utter despair, was overwhelming. One of the visiting UGIF doctors observed one little girl:

> She was sick. With her eyes glued to my face, she was begging me to ask the soldiers to let her go. She had been a good little girl all year; surely she didn't deserve to be put in prison.

As the children became increasingly restless, and their new playground began to look less attractive, the authorities gathered in their luxurious offices at the Avenue Foch to discuss their fate. The wide avenue, leading from the Arc de Triomphe and out towards the Bois de Boulogne, was lined with large chestnut trees, always heavy with leaves in July, and now throwing shadows onto the lawns and façades of the distinguished buildings all around. There was just one item on the agenda. What was to be done with the thousands of Jewish children who had been arrested?

In fact, Dannecker had already taken the initiative. A week earlier he had cabled Eichmann in Berlin, asking whether 'children under sixteen years of age could be deported after the fifteenth convoy.' An answer had still to be received. One French official proposed dispatching the children to orphanages run by UGIF, but Dannecker was anxious that they accompany their parents to the deportation camps at Pithiviers and Beaune-la-Rolande, pending the decision from Berlin.

And then came an unexpected intervention. Pierre Laval, no less a figure than the head of Marshal Pétain's government, let it be known to Helmut Knochen that he was not opposed to the deportation of the children of *La Grande Rafle*. Something altogether unexpected was happening: in the implementation of the 'Final Solution' of the Jewish problem, Vichy was ahead of the Reich. Even Dannecker was astonished, hastily dispatching another telegram to Berlin in which he could scarcely conceal his glee:

> Laval has proposed that children below the age of sixteen be included in the deportation of Jewish families from the free zone. The fate of Jewish children in the occupied zone does not interest him.

Never before had an occupied country co-operated with such evident enthusiasm.

On July 29, 1942, Eichmann telephoned from Berlin. Had there ever been any real doubt about his decision? Yes, the children could indeed be deported. Making a record of this telephone conversation, Dannecker noted:

> I have discussed the question of the deportation with SS-Obersturmbannführer Eichmann, and we came to the conclusion that as soon as it was possible to resume convoys to Germany, we would send children as well.

It was all quite simple really. Laval and his police made a specific proposition. Eichmann made a decision on it. Dannecker was still grateful for this unexpected initiative from the French. The paper-work was virtually complete. Now the children could be separated from their parents and taken to Drancy. French police were soon bludgeoning Jewish mothers into giving up their children. The mothers left first, the children followed. When they arrived in Drancy in a pitiful state, no one was there to comfort them. A Red Cross helper, Annette Monod, posted this last letter from a seven year old:

> Madame la concierge
> I am writing to you because I have nobody else. Last week Papa was deported. Mama has been deported. I have lost my purse. I have nothing left.

Within two weeks the time had come for the children to move on again. Now the machinery was unstoppable. Annette Monod was present as the children prepared to move on once more:

> The gendarmes tried to have a roll call. But children and names did not correspond. Rosenthal, Biegelmann, Radetski – it all meant nothing to them. They did not understand what was wanted of them, and several even wandered away from the group. That was how a little boy approached a gendarme, to play with the whistle hanging at his belt; a little girl made off to a small bank on which a few flowers were growing, and she picked some to make a bunch. The gendarmes did not know what to do. Then the order came to escort the children to the railway station nearby, without insisting on the roll call. The thing that mattered was to reach the right number overall. The place where we were was only about two hundred metres from the station. But the distance was made no shorter for these tots by their awkward bundles. That was when I saw a gendarme carry the miserable package of a wisp of a boy of four or five, for him to be better able to walk. But a warrant officer objected, shrieking at the gendarme on the grounds that a Frenchman in uniform does not carry the baggage of a Jew. Crestfallen, the gendarme gave the child back his package. I followed the column, my heart aching, unable to turn my back on these little children who had been in my care for a few weeks. I could hardly

restrain my tears, and I must say that many gendarmes also did not hide their feelings. When we reached the departure platform, I noticed that a German sentry, standing on a passageway above the station, had us covered with his machine gun. Getting onto the train then took place with an anxiety which had suddenly turned feverish.

The freight cars had no foot boards, and many of the children were too small to step up. The bigger ones climbed in first and helped pull in the smaller ones. The gendarmes lent a hand, taking the youngest, still babies in arms, and passing them to those already inside, among whom were a few women, indeed the few who were breast-feeding. Whereupon the children gave way to fear. They did not want to leave and began to sob, calling on the social workers and even the gendarmes to help them. I remember little Jacquet, aged five and especially endearing. Begging for my help he called out, 'I want to get down, I want to see the lady again, I don't want to do pipi here, I want the lady to help me down to do pipi . . .' The door of the wagon was closed and padlocked, but he still stuck his hand out through a crack between two planks; his fingers moved; he continued to cry out, 'I don't want to do pipi here, I want the lady to help me do pipi . . .' The warrant officer whom I have mentioned gave that hand a blow.

The children were mixed into convoys with adults, to make it seem as though families were being deported together. The young ones had invented a name for the fearful place for which they were bound. In Drancy it was known as 'Pitchipoi.' Yes, the children were off to Pitchipoi.

All of this was not enough for the Germans. *La Grande Rafle* had not been as *grande* as its planners had intended. Only 12,884 Jews had been seized: 9,800 on the first day and just over 3,000 on the second. It was something of a let-down. 'Operation Spring Wind' had set out to detain no fewer than 28,000 Jews. Yet thousands had escaped the net. Certain French police officers had proved less reliable than anticipated. And the people of Paris had also shown a measure of sympathy towards the victims, especially the children. There was a shortfall of well over 10,000 people.

Eichmann was not impressed. He had always had his doubts about France. Indeed when a deporting train once missed its schedule, Eichmann became extremely agitated and telephoned Dannecker's Judenreferat in Paris, threatening to drop France altogether as a country from which deportations would take place. Suddenly there loomed the humiliating prospect of France being excluded from Hitler's master plan. The Judenreferat pleaded with Eichmann. Its work had to be allowed to continue. On the strict understanding that not another train was to miss its schedule, Eichmann was persuaded to let the French programme continue. But as Dannecker's successor, Heinz Rothke so aptly put it: 'The programme can be achieved only if the French government makes a commitment to it with the necessary dynamism.'

Dannecker himself did not share his master's unease with the results of *La Grande Rafle*. At least the French had co-operated sufficiently to enable trains to roll. That had always been the priority. Shortly after the great round-up, Dannecker was recalled to Berlin. There was now other work for him to do.

The old Jewish quarter of Paris, whose history dates back to the Middle Ages, had been the central stage on which something quite unthinkable had been acted out. Ever since the French Revolution in 1789, it was to ancient streets like the rue du Roi-de-Sicile, the rue des Rosiers, and the rue des Blancs-Manteaux, that Jews had come; full of hope, energy and above all charged with the conviction that finally they would be free. But it was to these very streets that the 888 arrest teams had headed time and again.

One young mother and her son were actually helped out of the *Vélodrome d'Hiver* by a French policeman. An ordinary *flic*, Louis Petitjean, had been so overcome with remorse after arresting them, that he had set off to the *Vél d'Hiv* in an attempt to retrieve them. He was the only policeman in Paris to head back. The remaining 9,000 officers involved in *La Grande Rafle* somehow or other succeeded in restraining their remorse.

6

Friends

In occupied Paris one could never quite be sure who was a friend. At least the *rafles* had a strange kind of certainty, for of the Jews living in an *arrondissement* selected for a round-up, the chances were that some would be detained. The net of anti-Jewish legislation had by now been cast so thoroughly that every Jew risked arrest for violation of any one of the numerous and detailed provisions of those laws. A public park in which a stroll should not have been taken; shopping during proscribed hours; wearing the yellow star in a manner which failed to conform with the Eighth Ordinance. Nonetheless, with an uncanny combination of great prudence and even greater luck, thousands of Parisian Jews evaded the tentacles of Nazism. To this extent at least, they appeared to have some control over their lives.

But for those Jews who continued to walk the tortuous tightrope of life in occupied Paris, there lurked, unseen, a new and more ominous danger. Wherever a Jew went, whatever he did, whoever he was with, seldom did he have peace of mind. For somebody might already have denounced him. *Délation*, denunciation, brought continual anxiety to every Jew who had eluded the detention centre of Drancy. Thousands of anonymous letters had been pouring into the anti-Jewish police, who opened files and began inquiries. The following unsigned letter illustrates the nature of *délation:*

Since you are taking care of Jews, and if your campaign is not just a vain word, then have a look at the kind of life led by the girl M.A., formerly a dancer, now living at 31 Boulevard de Strasbourg, not wearing a star. This person, for whom being Jewish is not enough, debauches the husbands of proper Frenchwomen, and you may well have an idea what she is living off. Defend women against Jewishness – that will be your best publicity – and you will return a French husband to his wife.

The newspaper *Au Pilori* was always at hand to advise would-be informants. In fact, *délation* was simple, requiring only a letter to the Commissariat Générale aux Questions Juives. One such letter was written on the notepaper of the Ministry of the Interior:

> I have the honour to draw your attention, for whatever useful purposes it may serve, to the fact that an apartment at 57 *bis* Boulevard Rochechouart, belonging to the Jew Gresalmer, contains very fine furniture.

In 1940 alone, the Vichy and German authorities received between three and five million poison-pen letters. The informants, mostly invisible and anonymous, created an atmosphere of intimidation and despair that cast another shadow over the demoralized Jewish quarters of Paris.

By the end of 1942, more than 42,000 people had been deported from France, among them the children seized during *La Grande Rafle*. The deportation of 33,000 Jews within eleven weeks between July and September was only possible because of the co-operation of the French administration. No other country occupied by the Germans implemented such an enthusiastic policy of collaboration as Vichy France. True, the groundwork had been carefully prepared by Knochen, Lischka and Dannecker, yet they knew that it would have been impossible to proceed without French support.

*   *   *

Paulette Szlifke liked to think she knew who her friends were. Knowing who could be trusted was indispensable to the Resistance. The more she learned about the deportations, the more her resolve strengthened. Resistance had rapidly become a way of life. Solidarité had been established only two years earlier, in November 1940, with some fifty groups of workers functioning in and around the Jewish areas of Paris. At first, groups of five people each would gather to plot and plan. Now that the groups were down to three members, 'triangles' of resistants were scattered all over Paris. By 1943, Solidarité had established numerous sub-sections: groups of intellectuals, doctors, lawyers, for example, all prepared to use their specialist skills to help the movement.

Paulette Szlifke belonged to the movement's youth section, L'Organisation de la Jeunesse Juive, the Organization of Jewish Youth, which worked closely with a number of other underground groups. Although these youngsters were steeped in Jewish culture, and their background was that of Jewish clubs and organizations, they were essentially French and distinctly proud of it. Their clandestine journal, *En Avant*, was printed not in the Yiddish of their immigrant parents, but in French, and every page was filled with the defiant language of French nationalism.

The work of the Resistance was not for the faint-hearted, and that of the youth section was not child's play. Every illicit rendezvous was fraught with danger and the threat of deception was ever-present. Many of Paulette's colleagues had already been shot, deported or detained. Within her triangle, each resistant was responsible for '*politique*,' '*matériel*,' or organization. Paulette was in charge of '*matériel*,' which meant that she organized the transportation of tracts, deployed poster teams, and prepared literature for distribution in blocks of flats, at factory gates, on the Métro or at the cinema; in fact, wherever people gathered and might be receptive to the message of the Resistance. Every day the three members would agree upon a fixed time to meet, and if for some reason one failed to arrive, the meeting would automatically be carried forward to the next day.

The Resistance movement was always on the look-out for potential members charged with defiance, hope and energy. In many respects Lucienne Kornberg seemed an ideal new recruit.

Like Paulette Szlifke, she was Jewish and lived in the run-down eleventh *arrondissement*, in the rue des Immeubles Industrielles, a stone's throw from the rue de Vaucouleurs. Lucienne's parents had been detained in a *rafle*, and now, in the early spring of 1943, were in Drancy awaiting a decision on their fate. The nineteen-year-old girl was understandably determined to do whatever she could to help the Resistance.

Lucienne's credentials seemed excellent, but checks would still have to be made. At a second meeting, her story remained unchanged: she was prepared to take risks and eager to participate in 'actions.' During a final meeting, Lucienne revealed that she had an impeccable contact who could be of great benefit to Solidarité; someone who could remove the seals now attached to the hundreds of apartments officially closed after the round-up of their occupants; a true friend to the Jews. She then disclosed that her contact was an ordinary French *flic*, a policeman. Not surprisingly, suspicion was aroused.

To reconcile the girl's contacts with the police with her desire to work for Solidarité was extremely difficult. There were, in fact, 'flics' in the Resistance, but they certainly did not broadcast their activities. Yet if the girl had anything to hide, why did she flaunt her police contact? There would have to be further investigations.

Paulette Szlifke was to pose as the daughter of a family which had been deported, ostensibly seeking access to the family home to gather a few possessions. The two young women met for the first time, and again Lucienne's story remained consistent. Like her colleagues, Paulette was very suspicious. Moreover, she spotted what should have been obvious earlier: Lucienne Kornberg was having an intimate relationship with the policeman.

When Paulette went with Lucienne to the girl's apartment, Lucienne proudly displayed gifts from the doting policeman. Later, when the two young women parted at the Place de la Nation, Lucienne walked over to a man sitting alone on a bench. They appeared to know one another, but it was impossible to determine the precise nature of their relationship. It was after the meeting between Lucienne and the man that Paulette began to suspect that she was being followed. Her life had become so bizarre that she was tempted to spot conspiracy everywhere, and this was not the first time that she had thought that someone was on her tail. However, aware that her imagination could play tricks, she wondered if this latest suspicion was a delusion.

The Jews of France were in the forefront of resistance to the Nazis. Of the thousand people executed in the prison of Mont Valérien, 160 were Jewish, even though Jews numbered less than one per cent of the general population. The fact that many Jewish Resistants were prepared to give their lives to liberate France was not appreciated by the French public as a whole. On the contrary, certain French anti-Semites had been quick to use the press to defend measures that discriminated against the Jews. A *Paris-Soir* journalist put it thus:

I saw them, those millionaire Jews, interned near Paris . . . lined up in front of us we recognized them, the celebrities of the former Jewish bar: M. Théodore Valensi, M. Maurice Weill-Raynal, M. Edmond Boch, M. Crémieuz . . . All lawyers, politicians, powerful and respected. Justice at last!

*　　　*　　　*

It was six o'clock in the morning. There was a knock at the door. As soon as she heard that unexpected sound, Paulette Szlifke leapt out of bed and began stuffing into her mouth four pieces of thin cigarette paper. On these were written the addresses of sympathizers with Solidarité who had provided money rather than mere encouragement. Still half asleep, she was trying to swallow when the front door was barged down with a loud crash. She swallowed again in a desperate attempt to consume this unexpected breakfast, and this time was successful. Six burly officers of the Brigade Spéciale, the anti-terrorist branch of the police, immediately began to conduct a search of her meagre room.

Hiding places for her papers were scarce, and she had never made any serious attempt at concealment. Within minutes, a pile of Resistance tracts was retrieved from beneath her bed. They had been due for distribution later that evening. Few words were spoken. Fragile and frightened, Paulette Szlifke was escorted away. Was it her turn to receive the death sentence? Penal policy in occupied France was invariably harsh, and her mind turned to the plight of a fellow Resistant, Dakovski, who had perished barely a year earlier. The young electrician, who lived in the eighteenth *arrondissement* had been sentenced to death for armed resistance. His last letter, reproduced in full here, gives an indication of what motivated the young fighter and of the flavour of the Resistance movement:

> Paris
> La Santé Prison
> June 4, 1942
> The last day of my life

To my dear little mother, to my dear father,

Of course you'll know that I've been condemned to death. It's 9 o'clock in the morning and I've just been told that my appeal for clemency has been rejected since I've been condemned to death on two counts. The execution is due to take place today. After today I'll no longer be on this earth. You must, dear father, you must be full of courage and support mum in the pain which I know I'm inflicting on her. Actually I'm relatively calm and peaceful at this moment, and can look death right in the eye since I know I've done nothing to be ashamed of in this life. I've always been a hard worker. I know I've sometimes been unfair towards you and towards mum; I therefore now ask you to pardon me; dear dad, we've had our rows, but I hope now that all that is behind us. I do beg you both, mum and dad, not to be too sad and to bring up my young brother, Jean, as you have done for me, to be an honest and hard working man; and do try to ensure that he becomes a good worker and that he at least gets some qualifications by going to evening classes.

I did have plans for the future, for when the war ends; I had wanted to open a shop; to have children whom you would love; but now you'll have to channel all your affections into our young Michel, the younger son of Céline and Sylvian, your grand-children. I know that you will have plenty of grief but you must try to be brave. Please don't think that I'm at all happy about the prospect of leaving you all. Destiny has decreed that I should not attain my twenty-fifth year. You've made so many sacrifices in bringing me up and now, when I should be in a position to pay you back, I have to leave you. What is to be done? Such is destiny. Over these last days, I have been thinking of all the wonderful dishes that mum would prepare for me, her spoiled child, and I can still savour those tastes which linger on in my memory.

I've asked some friends who I met in court to give you my address in prison. I also asked if I would be able to receive a parcel and was told that, as an exception, I could. But you have to bring it this morning. In any case, it's not that important, my dear little mum, if you haven't been able to bring anything. I've got the right to write three letters, so I'm going to write one to my aunt, and the other two sheets will be for you. It's a fine day today. I thought I would die on a lovely day. Mum, I do plead with you to be strong. Above all, do try to eat well – and make sure that dad does likewise. I know I've been a spoiled child, but one must overcome . . .[illegible]

On July 10 you'll be able to collect my personal effects, but only by paying what's due in advance. Everything that's in my room belongs to me. If you go along to the Kommandantur, or to La Santé Prison, the prison will be best I think, you'll be able to get my things, and the 345 francs which I had on me when I was arrested. You should also see my boss since he owes me four days' money. I believe that he owes me for them, and you might also ask him if he can't give you my holiday money. All that I've

been able to save is for you. If you have any problems
access to my room, you can always seek the autho
the Kommandantur. They'll allow this for someon
been shot.

If you wish to have a picture of me enlarged or f
my best photo is my most recent one in which I'
jacket. I believe that Louise had one which she'll
Do copy out this letter within a few days since t
pencil will soon fade, and you'll no longer have
me. You might also remake my suit for Jeannot
he could well do with. I haven't mentioned eve
I just haven't got the space, but please do pa
colleagues and friends that while I've been he
been thinking of each and every one of them.
exactly what I was up to, but one day you v
able to hold your head up high because I am d
knowing why and for what I've been fighting
to the idea that my ideal . . . [illegible] . .
death, I am proud to die for my country ar
in which there'll be no more of man's ir
don't expect you to take in all of this ju
you will.

Before dying I am asking my brother
with mum and dad, and to help them
moment; and do remember that mon
which makes for happiness. I've thoug
who cooks such delicious dishes, an
whom I've eaten and spent such goo
of little Yvette's father as well as al
name here owing to lack of space,
much with me in my thoughts. I ar
my dear parents. This letter is a li
what I wanted to say.

Farewell, darling mum, be ch
proud; farewell dad, Jean, Marc
Céline.

It
th
w
of
Su
ma
her
just
par
P
of a
Mar
gers.
and
that
interr
for its
Afte
where
Widely
hatred
particul
of form
extract i
to threa
Paulette
appeared

Marcel – help dad to get over these rough times. Think of me every June 4, and have a special meal. This, then, is my last word. Lots of love. Farewell. It's midday and they are waiting for me. Goodbye mum; goodbye dad. With love to you all.

Vive la France!

*　　　*　　　*

was still not quite light. The police van pulled up outside e Prefecture of Police opposite the Hôtel-Dieu. Paulette Szlifke s taken up to the fifth floor and whisked through a series colourless corridors. A door was opened into a large room. ddenly, she was no longer alone, for there before her were ny fellow-Resistants. Not just the young boy and girl from triangle, but dozens of other Solidarité workers too. And not Solidarité members: the room was packed with Communists, isans and others opposed to the Reich.

ulette was enormously relieved to see her friends, but instead knowledging them she decided to adopt once more her alias as e-Thérèse Muldaise, pretending to be among complete stran- The room contained several benches set out with precision single bed in the left-hand corner. It soon became clear he bed was reserved for the last person to emerge from gation. Paulette silently rehearsed her role, bracing herself most rigorous test.

r well over an hour, she was called into the adjacent room, sat Commissaire David, the head of the Brigade Spéciale. and ironically known as 'David le Rouge,' because of his of Communists, the Commissaire was reputed to be a arly vicious sadist. His speciality was crushing the testicles er fighters in the International Brigades, not in order to nformation, but simply for pleasure. Nor would he hesitate en to execute the spouse of a prisoner who refused to talk. knew immediately who faced her, and Commissaire David to know something about her, too.

During the first interrogation, and indeed those that followed, Commissaire David repeatedly put one simple question: 'What is the significance of number 34 rue de Vaucouleurs?' The first reference to the workshop where her parents remained in hiding sent shivers down Paulette's spine. Realizing that she must have been followed coming and going from that address, her answers were confident and clear, at least to begin with. There must have been a mistake. She had never been there. When the police photographer took her 'mugshot,' Paulette could not withhold a faint, sardonic smile. Commissaire David decided that his officers would go to number 34, since he had not got any sense from the young prisoner.

*　　*　　*

Yentyl and Efrayim Szlifke had become experts on the acoustics of the block which now served to imprison them. Suddenly they heard new and strange voices. Two police officers were downstairs questioning the concierge, 'Do you know this person? She is a terrorist,' as they clutched the photograph of Paulette. The concierge recognized her and promptly panicked, saying the first thing that entered her head: 'Yes, I know that girl, but she doesn't live here, she lives at number 14, just along the road,' and indicating the direction of the apartment where the Szlifkes used to live.

Thanking the woman, the policeman and his colleague rushed off to the nearby address.

Yentyl and Efrayim had overheard the whole conversation. There was only one thing to do: make a run for it. The concierge was storming towards the workshop.

'Get out of here immediately,' she shrieked, on arriving, 'terrorists, terrorists.' But her lodgers-in-hiding needed no coercion and hurried off in the opposite direction to number 14. Within minutes, they had bumped into a neighbour, who ushered them to an address where other Jews were in hiding. The Szlifkes would be able to stay there for the moment at least.

Moments later the fumbling policemen were back from number

83

14, where they had found an apartment which had been officially sealed. They had finally discovered Efrayim Szlifke's secret workshop. The concierge hastily denied all knowledge of anyone ever having been there, adding that she was as amazed as the police were. Unintentionally, she had helped her two hideaways.

*   *   *

Paulette had been at the Prefecture for almost a week when the police bungled their detective work in the rue de Vaucouleurs. Forced to interrogate her again, Commissaire David was not amused. It was time for a different ploy:

> 'So your parents live at number 34. Nothing to be ashamed of about that. We have nothing against the Jews, you know. But we have arrested your parents all the same.'
>
> 'And what about my brother Robert?' snapped back the defiant prisoner.
>
> 'Yes, we've taken him in too. You see, it would have been much easier for you to have talked in the first place. Then all of our little chats would have been unnecessary.'

At a stroke Paulette Szlifke had succeeded in calling the bluff of one of the most experienced interrogators in Paris. Now she knew that her parents were probably still in hiding. For Robert Szlifke had been away from Paris for almost a year and could not have been arrested, at least not in that city.

The police had been expecting to uncover a major cache of Resistance weapons at number 34 and were angered and frustrated at having found nothing more than a tatty old furrier's workshop. Paulette Szlifke would have to pay for their failure. Commissaire David wielded a large truncheon, while two other interrogating officers in turn whipped the young girl until she was almost unconscious. Still she refused to give any information about her work in the Resistance. To betray colleagues was unthinkable.

Now it was Paulette's turn to lie on the single bed. There had been another series of raids throughout the city and there were a few new faces in the large room on the fifth floor. Among this new haul was a young Catholic doctor, who went over to the badly battered girl. Quietly, she suggested that Paulette make a formal request for medical attention. Without speaking, Paulette indicated that she was grateful for the advice, although privately she knew the idea was a waste of time. But later, as her body started to reveal a pattern of blue bruises, she began to reconsider the doctor's suggestion. At worst her request would be refused.

After eight days at the Prefecture, Szlifke was taken away for another round of interrogation. The terrifying routine had become familiar. This time, though, she was the first to speak, immediately asking to see a doctor. To her surprise, the request was granted.

Paulette Szlifke had scored one small victory: she was to be escorted by two policemen to the Hôtel-Dieu Hospital opposite, where she would be examined by a qualified doctor. The doctor asked the two policemen to leave the room. At once, Paulette begged him for help:

'Please, they are accusing me of being a terrorist – and if I'm left here a day longer those bastards are going to kill me.'

There was not time to enter into a protracted explanation. It was a straightforward plea for help.

'Madamoiselle,' replied the doctor in a loud voice, 'I regret to have to tell you that you have a severe inflammation in and around your genital area and it is in my opinion an immediate case for hospitalization.'

The two officers waiting outside were informed of the patient's condition. Giving strict orders that on no account was she to be left alone, one officer left to seek further instructions from Commissaire David. The prisoner was to be escorted immediately to the Rothschild Hospital.

On her way to the hospital, Paulette Szlifke thought of Lucienne Kornberg, who had clearly betrayed her. The Prefecture had been ringing with Lucienne's name, and dozens of Solidarité workers had been similarly denounced. In occupied Paris one really could not be sure who was a friend.

7

A Most Unusual Operation

No one could denounce Armand Kohn. The threat of *délation* posed no threat to him. Silent enemies might try, but their endeavours would be thwarted. Every aspect of Kohn's existence was strictly in accordance with the law. As chief administrator of the Rothschild Hospital, he was entitled to keep on his person a *carte de légitimation*. Kohn's card read as follows:

M: KOHN Armand
Function in UGIF: Administrator at the Rothschild Hospital
. . . is hereby exempt from all measures of internment. This protection extends and applies to any family member living with him. This authorizing document is issued in accordance with the requirements of the occupying authorities. The relevant German authorities are in possession of a copy of this document.

Armand Kohn always made doubly sure that his card was safely inside his wallet before setting off for the Rothschild Hospital at eight-thirty each morning. Here was the piece of paper which would guarantee the safety and unity of his family. His policy of cautious co-operation, constantly criticized by those around him, appeared to have paid off.

Every day a chauffeur would drive Kohn to the hospital at Picpus. Kohn's eldest son Philippe was a student at l'Essec; one daughter, Rose-Marie, attended a music conservatoire, while the other, Antoinette, was a university student. The youngest son, Georges-André, now eleven, was a boarder at Gerson College, a prestigious private school outside the capital. He was doing particularly well; not only was he extremely diligent and hard-working, he was also recognized by pupils and teachers as the brightest pupil of his year. Armand's mother and his wife Suzanne were likewise at liberty, living very much as they had done before the Germans arrived. How many other Jewish families could display such an impressive hand three years after the installation of a regime so hostile to the Jews?

The Rothschild Hospital continued to prescribe its bizarre form of medicine. Bizarre, because it aimed not to cure and discharge patients but to prolong their stay so as to forestall what recovery inevitably led to: a return to Drancy. From the end of 1941, the Rothschild had become a prison-hospital for the Jews. The traditional brand of hospital administration had long since gone, and the Prefecture of Police and the Prefecture of the Seine now shared responsibility for the institution. A notice attached to the barbed wire surrounding the hospital made it clear that even well-wishers were unwelcome:

> It is expressly forbidden for people outside to speak or communicate with the sick detained here and who are within the prohibited zone. Any breach of this regulation will lead to immediate arrest.

There were two separate pavilions for the detained: 'Medicine' and 'Surgery.' Both contained Jews, but every now and then a non-Jew was admitted. Dannecker had once been infuriated by the presence of a Swiss patient in the surgical pavilion who, when pressed by his SS inquisitor, revealed that he did not feel in the least dishonoured by sharing a ward with Jews. Dannecker's response was to have a notice bearing the words 'Honorary Jew' suspended over the patient's bed.

When a new patient arrived at the Rothschild all personal effects, and in particular the patient's shoes and money, were confiscated to discourage any attempts to abscond.

Armand Kohn had no qualms about his role within UGIF. Disqualified by decree from working in his own field, he had simply been asked to do a different job. He was the closest, indeed the only, relative of the Rothschilds who had chosen to remain in Paris throughout the war. In any case, for some time UGIF did appear to provide a last refuge for many Parisian Jews. UGIF, with its administrative council of eighteen, was believed by its Jewish members to be a foundation dedicated to the help of their troubled compatriots. And yet Armand had failed to see that it had long been the Germans' intention to get the Jews themselves to collaborate in Berlin's carefully crafted plan. It was a technique which had proved itself time and again. As Dannecker himself put it:

> From our experience in Germany and the protectorates of Bohemia and Moravia, it is clear that by excluding the Jews from a number of spheres of daily life, their segregation into a distinct and separate class follows inevitably.

From the beginning, UGIF had been constructed by the Germans, not to protect the interests of French Jewry, but to speed their eventual elimination. While Father Paul Vergara had dubbed UGIF 'an infamous trap disguised as a pro-Jewish organization,' Kohn remained unaware that he was venturing deeper and deeper into that trap.

In the spring of 1943 what weighed most heavily on Kohn's mind was how to carry out his job effectively. The efficient completion of a task always gave him considerable pleasure. He was an administrator and a thoroughly efficient one. It was his task to ensure that there were no more unauthorized departures from the two pavilions housing detainees. There had been three further successful escapes from the hospital and one thwarted attempt. It was certainly not Kohn's intention to act as a jailer, but he knew very well that the Germans would exact far-reaching reprisals should anyone else escape.

Arbitrary round-ups and ward clearances had already taken place by way of retribution. Kohn therefore considered it essential to secure the blocks housing detainees. It was all very well for those who succeeded in escaping, but others, less able or less inclined to break out, also deserved a degree of protection.

The difficult issue of hospital security had been on Kohn's mind for some time. A year earlier, in April of 1942, he had met with senior police officials in the grounds of the hospital itself. The agenda contained only one item: how to prevent escapes. Even at that time it had been obvious that new measures would have to be introduced. Therefore the basement was sealed off more effectively; the lift mechanism was modified to prevent it descending to the basement; and there followed tighter policing of the two pavilions.

All windows were kept closed at night and, most humiliating of all for the patients, night attire was no longer issued. As a result of this last ruling, ghostly inmates paraded around covered in nothing but a sheet. Kohn let it be known that he would draft further and more restrictive measures if necessary. He was determined that his plans should be carried out as comprehensively as anything else to which he had applied himself in the past.

*   *   *

On March 30, 1943, the hospital registrar made his seven hundred and sixty-first entry of the year. The new patient was to be assigned to Pavilion number 4, on the first floor, where all the women in 'Medicine' were to be found. But the particulars of entry number 761 were unlike the others, for they were in bold red ink, indicating that the detainee had been sent from the Prefecture of Police. Seven-six-one was Paulette Szlifke. Her most pressing problem was the absence of a genuine medical condition, other than her flagging spirits. The Rothschild may well have been the most peculiar hospital in the land, with armed guards patrolling its well-tended gardens, but its medical personnel at least attempted to help those who happened to come under their jurisdiction.

However, the hospital was buzzing with rumours that the Head of Surgery was collaborating unreservedly with the Germans –

most bizarre since he was a Jew. Others in the hospital continued to defy the Reich. Paulette was aware that within the hospital there was a cluster of doctors and employees who were active in the Resistance, but it was very difficult to make contact with the right people. After Lucienne Kornberg, she was reluctant to trust anyone. Nonetheless, Paulette knew that it was imperative to renew contact with her superiors in the Resistance. As the only person to have emerged from the Prefecture without going to Drancy, she knew that her colleagues could benefit from her inside knowledge.

While biding her time and wondering who to approach, Paulette was herself approached. A doctor Lobelson had seen from the Registrar's book that she had come from the Prefecture and was a political detainee. He indicated that he too was a member of Solidarité, and would do all he could to help. Messages from outside confirmed that this was true.

Before long Lobelson had come up with an idea. He would do everything within his power to assist Paulette to escape from the hospital. He told her that six weeks' convalescence was required by French law, but that to qualify for it the patient had to have undergone surgery. It would be relatively straightforward to diagnose a case of acute appendicitis and there would be nothing to suspect. It was Lobelson's intention to effect the escape some time during Paulette's recuperation. Paulette knew that if she was to avoid Drancy, then Lobelson's strategy was the only way out of the Rothschild. She did not relish the prospect of undergoing bogus surgery, but it was her only option.

After some three weeks in the medical pavilion, Paulette was moved to the surgical division headed by Dr Hertz, the alleged collaborator. The operation was scheduled for 10 pm on April 20, 1943. On that day Paulette Szlifke suddenly began to have grave doubts about the wisdom of Lobelson's plan. A perfectly healthy young girl was about to be rendered unconscious, cut open, have a part of her anatomy removed, and then be stitched up again, all in the hope that she might be able to escape at some as yet unspecified time.

A MOST UNUSUAL OPERATION

Since this day might be her last, there was only one sensible thing to do: to enjoy every moment left to her. Paulette had not the slightest doubt about how she should spend those few remaining hours. She would consume anything sweet which remained in her possession. Recalling that when she had been arrested she had some special-category food coupons known as 'J3s,' which entitled youngsters to rations of chocolate, Paulette decided that the time could not have been more appropriate for an impromptu feast. Moreover, a kindly nurse had smuggled for her some additional coupons. Having traded in her 'J3s', she set about gorging herself on the carefully counted chocolates. Paulette was not disappointed, as she savoured her last, lonely banquet.

As the hour of the operation approached, Paulette recalled Lobelson's instruction: her mind was not to be filled with any thought which might betray their plan. Any mention of Solidarité as she regained consciousness after the operation would be disastrous for them both. As chloroform was administered, Paulette embarked on a silent ritual, repeating to herself: 'My mind is empty and I am thinking of nothing.'

*　　*　　*

The Rothschild Hospital contained a maternity wing. Most of the women admitted were in the advanced stages of their pregnancies and had been transferred from Drancy. The women were allowed to stay at the hospital until they had given birth, after which both mother and newborn child were simply returned to the internment camp.

The midwives at the hospital did what they could to prolong the stay of the young mothers, usually by fabricating a variety of infantile fevers and colics. Several tragic scenes occurred, for whenever there was a successful escape from the hospital, the Germans had no compunction in taking to Drancy, in reprisal, an entire ward of mothers and babies. The more escapes, the more reprisals. The maternity wing was always top of the list for such measures.

Dr Hertz, the head of the hospital's surgical division, continued to astound colleagues and inmates alike. Unprompted by Armand Kohn, or indeed by the German authorities, he had nailed large planks of wood to the doors of his pavilion, which he then bolted for good measure. He showed such zeal in transferring to Drancy all patients under his jurisdiction that he could deliver a rate of dispatch which not even the Germans were demanding. He once performed a hysterectomy on a Mrs Lubin, who, after the operation, continued to suffer greatly. Dr Hertz nonetheless deemed that she was fit enough to leave the hospital and be returned to Drancy. When a colleague pointed out that the woman in the bed next to Mrs Lubin was by comparison hardly ill, having only a minor chest infection, the doctor's response showed consistency if nothing else: he ensured that both ladies left immediately for Drancy.

*　　　*　　　*

Paulette's greatest fear as she regained consciousness was that she would reveal all she knew about Solidarité. But her silent command to herself appeared to have worked. Her most nightmarish thought had been a bizarre image of Commissaire David sitting at the foot of her bed taking copious notes laden with contact numbers and passwords. Nothing so fanciful had happened. Then, as the effects of the chloroform began to fade, the young Resistance fighter cried out, 'I want my mummy, I want my mummy,' her desperate plea echoing around the corridors of the hospital. An understanding nurse rushed to her, anxious to offer comfort.

'If you would like to see your mother, just tell us where she is and we'll do our very best to contact her and arrange that she comes to see you.'

There were strict and detailed regulations governing who could see who and when; but the prospect of a visit by Yentyl Szlifke was the last thing likely to happen. In any case, Paulette did not like the nurse's tone; it smacked of the Prefecture. Could she be trusted? One of the Commissaire's informers perhaps?

'No. No. I will not tell you where my mother is,' replied Paulette, still barely conscious.

The nurse said nothing.

'But,' said the young patient, 'I want to see my mummy anyway.'

In fact Paulette's parents had so far succeeded in eluding the Germans. After their hasty departure from the rue de Vaucouleurs, Solidarité was able to supply Efrayim and Yentyl with a series of addresses. It was not safe to remain long in one place.

As Paulette Szlifke recovered, she began to compile reports and to send them via Lobelson to colleagues in Solidarité. There were six weeks in which to prepare, plan and execute her escape from the hospital. She knew that, because of the extraordinary measures taken by Dr Hertz, her task had been made all the more precarious and that time was not on her side.

Ten days after the operation Paulette was feeling much better. Another few days and she would be back in shape. These thoughts were interrupted by Dr Lobelson. Extremely agitated as he hurried towards Paulette's bed, he tried to calm himself before blurting out:

'The Germans are in the hospital. Hertz has said that you are ready to leave. You're to be signed out this morning.'

He then disappeared without attempting to explain, comfort or pacify. Minutes later he was back. He had been down to the kitchens and prepared a box of provisions for his fellow-Resistant.

'Take this. You may need it. I don't know where you are going, but take it anyway. Now you take care of yourself, see.'

Lobelson hurried off again.

An hour or so later a nurse arrived with an official explanation of sorts. It had been decided that Paulette was fit enough to leave the hospital. Her bed was now required. Slowly, Paulette got dressed. Surely the removal of her appendix had not been a waste of time?

*   *   *

Adolf Eichmann was convinced that France was sluggish in dealing with the Jewish problem. Despite repeated assurances from those responsible, there continued to be a series of inexplicable delays in the deportation programme. Since Dannecker's departure from France, momentum had been lost. Eichmann's remedy was to send to Paris his own right-hand man, SS-Hauptsturmführer Aloïs Brünner. The instructions were unequivocal: the deportations were to be accelerated. Eichmann even travelled to Paris to ensure that his protégé was properly installed.

From his very first day in the French capital, Aloïs Brünner enjoyed great independence. He had brought with him a special detachment of twenty-five Austrian SS men and a fleet of cars. It was reminiscent of Knochen's entry into Paris in June of 1940. However, by receiving his orders directly from Eichmann, Brünner was to elude Knochen's authority.

One inmate of Drancy described Brünner thus:

. . . small, badly built, puny, with a look that gave away nothing, but wicked little eyes. His monotonous voice hardly ever rose. Perfidious, pitiless, a liar, he was unmoved by the dignified attitudes of his victims, their uprightness and good faith. In contrast, he cynically exploited human weaknesses and had no scruples about resorting to the most blatant blackmail, in other words deportation, to achieve his ends. He hit people rarely and without savagery but ostensibly affected physical repugnance of Jews.

The trains had to roll more frequently, with more Jews on board. Aloïs Brünner set about his task with determination. He would spend night and day scanning lists, construing as Jewish those previously classified as half-Jewish, so obsessed was he by the desire to fulfil his brief.

When Brünner arrived in Paris in June of 1943, it was with blood on his hands. Barely five months earlier he had been dispatched to the German zone of Salonika in Greece. This was another posting by Eichmann and one in which Brünner had excelled. He had been let loose on the Jewish community of the ancient Greek city. At first, Brünner's presence had not been understood by Greek Jewry, but his mission soon became clear: to deport the maximum number of Jews in the minimum amount of time. In Salonika the process was indeed accomplished with great speed. Under the command of Maximilian Merten, Brünner signed the deportation orders of tens of thousands of Greek Jews. He was frequently seen at work, whipping unco-operative prisoners, a revolver in each hand. By the middle of May, the last of the conscripts had been moved, making a total of 46,091 deportees. The thirty-one-year-old Austrian was obviously the ideal man to head the Gestapo's anti-Jewish commando unit in France.

SS-Hauptsturmführer Aloïs Brünner was born in the village of Rohrbrunn in the spring of 1912. On his nineteenth birthday he received full membership of the then secret Austrian Nazi Party, an honour he had hankered after for some time. A year later he entered the police school at Graz. Membership of the Austrian Legion followed and by 1938 he had come under the influence of Eichmann, joining the SS in that year as member number 342767. Brünner became Eichmann's personal secretary and in 1940–41 they arranged the deportation of 56,000 Viennese Jews.

One such unfortunate was the financier Siegmund Bosel. During the second night of their train journey to the East, Brünner chained Bosel to the floor of the wagon, berating his prisoner for being a profiteer. The old man repeatedly pleaded with the SS officer. When Brünner tired of tormenting Bosel, he drew his pistol and shot him dead. He then entered an adjoining carriage and asked if anyone had heard anything. After receiving various assurances that nothing had been heard, Brünner appeared to be satisfied.

From his very earliest days Brünner was noted for his combination of zest and cruelty. His sadistic streak appeared to be complemented by both administrative flair and genuine enthusiasm for the job. Brünner served in one of the SS Sonderkommandos, with the rank of Obersturmbannführer. His brutality in Minsk and other east European cities did much for his reputation in the eyes of his SS masters. Promotion to the rank of SS-Hauptsturmführer in January of 1942 was largely a formality. When Aloïs Brünner was posted to France in June of the following year, his brutal reputation preceded him.

Above: *Paulette Szlifke (left) with her parents Efrayim and Yentyl and younger brother Robert.*

Left: *Young mothers with their new-born babies in the maternity wing of the Rothschild Hospital. Most were deported – sometimes to fill Brünner's quotas, at other times by way of retribution.*

Right: *Aloïs Brünner at the time of his subscription to the Nazi Party.*

Below: *Some of those – among them Paulette Szlifke – who were sent on Brünner's first convoy.*

STEINER	EVA			
STEINERT	KARL			
STELZER	BRONISLAWA			
STERN	ISIDORE			
STIBBE	DAGOBERT			
STOKFISZ	CECILE			
STOKFISZ	MARJEM			
STRYKER	MOZES			
STURM	BERTHE			
STURM	SALOMON			
SVARTZ	MADELEINE			
SVARTZ	SOPHIE			
SZADMAN	ICEK		.82	SEJNY	P	WEISSHAAR
SZAFER	ICEK	.99	MOGELNICA	F	WEISZBERG
SZDACHOLZ	SMUL		PARIS		WILEZYNSKI
SZEJMAN	BEILA	11.04.24	LODZ	P	WINOCOUR
SZEJWACZ	ABRAHAM	14.07.05	LODZ	IND	WINOCOUR
SZLIFKE	PAULETTE	06.10.97	SCHLEIFMUHL	P	DE WINTER
SZPINER	ADELE	22.01.31	SWOLIN	P	WISZNIAK
SZRETER	CECILE	12.12.94	LODZ	P	WIZNITZER
SZTARKMAN	ABRAHAM	15.08.26	LODZ	P	WOLBERG
SZTARKMAN	ADELE	26.06.29	TOMATCHAVA	P	WOLBERG
SZTARKMAN	BERTHA	10.12.94	VARSOVIE	P	WOLKOWICZ
SZTARKMAN	MAURICE	05.07.23	BENDERINE	R	WOLLENBERGER
SZTARKMAN	MENACHIM	06.01.95	TULEZYN	P	WORONOFF
SZWARCENBERG	RYWEN	15.09.83	KRASNIK	P	WORTRAJCH
SZWARCMANN	MALKA	.85	KRASIK	F	WORTZMANN
TASZLICKI	NATHANIEL	25.05.86	VARSOVIE	F	YAKAR
TENENWURCEL	GITLA	.87	VARSOVIE	P	ZACHARIASZ
TENENWURCEL	ZEHMANN	27.03.83	DOBRZYN	P	ZACHARIASZ
TOKARZ	ITTA	07.08.17	VARSOVIE	P	ZAJDEMAN
TOKARZ	VICTOR	19.01.93	KARKHOFF	F	ZAJDEMAN
TOPOL	RUCHLA	19.04.83	PARIS	G	ZAJDENBERG
TRABSKA	EDWIG	18.04.23	SALONIQUE	IND	ZAJONC
TRABSKI	WLADIMIR	03.11.19	LEIPZIG	IND	ZAMECZKOWSK
TRUGMAN	ROGER	20.10.10	VARSOVIE	B	ZECKENDORF
TSENIO	ELIA	16.08.01	LOOZLAVILLE	HOL	ZECKENDORF
URBACH	BERNARD	25.08.99	AMSTERDAM	HOL	ZECKENDORF
URTICU	PERLA	07.12.23	AMSTERDAM	B	ZEDEMAN
VAN AALTER	JEAN	25.06.04			
	LOUIS				

On their descent from the train – towards the gas chambers.
Even the children were not spared.

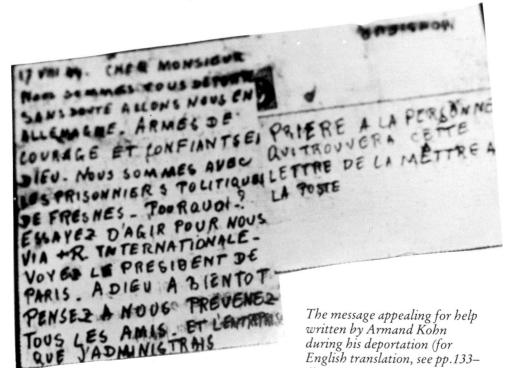

The message appealing for help written by Armand Kohn during his deportation (for English translation, see pp.133–4).

Right: *A sketch of Armand Kohn drawn by a friend during their incarceration at Buchenwald.*

Below: *Armand's telegram to his son Philippe, announcing the loss of his wife and daughter at Bergen-Belsen.*

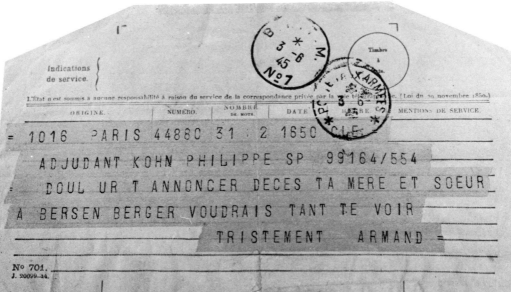

Left: *Arnold Strippel: alive and well and living today in the Federal Republic of Germany.*

Below: *Searching for the missing children: photographs pinned to the wall of the Hotel Lutetia after the war.*

Left: *Georges-André Kohn at the time of his first communion, in Paris.*

Below: *Two years later: the same boy, now the subject of vile medical experiments at the concentration camp of Neuengamme.*

TOP NAZI FOUND

Alois Brunner, aged 73, the most important Nazi war criminal still at large, may be on the point of being discreetly expelled from Syria, according to French Nazi hunter Serge Klarsfeld, *Robin Smyth reports from Paris.* Brunner (above), accused of the deportation of 150,000 Austrian, German, French, Greek and East European Jews, is—Klarsfeld says—more significant than Klaus Barbie, whose trial in France is due to start next year. Tracked down by the German magazine *Bunte* last week, Brunner lost an eye and part of his left hand opening Israeli letter bombs. France, Austria and Germany have applied for his extradition.

Above: *Philippe Kohn (second from right) speaking at a meeting to campaign for Strippel's prosecution. On the far left are Serge and Beate Klarsfeld.*

Left: *Reports of the imminent arrest of Brünner are frequent, but so far, none has been borne out.*

over the faces of those unfortunates he tormented. As the stunned doctors slowly returned to their pavilions, Brünner moved on to the next item of his informal agenda. He now wanted to see the chief administrator.

Armand Kohn presented himself. Old enough to be the young Hauptsturmführer's father, Kohn nonetheless trembled from within. Now it was his turn to be put through his paces. Unlike most of the other doctors, Kohn was fluent in German, a language which he had absorbed effortlessly as a child.

'Are there any Aryans in your hospital?' enquired the SS man.

'Yes.'

'Why are they here?'

Considering this first interrogatory fairly predictable, Kohn nonetheless surprised himself with the outward firmness and confidence of his response:

'Some of them, those who are sick but free, because they want to be; others – the prisoners – because they have been brought here by the French police.'

'Don't you find it outrageous that there are Aryans here who are co-habiting with Jews?'

'Well . . .'

Kohn began to splutter out a reply, his earlier confidence shaken by the venom from the SS man. In any case, there was not the opportunity to give a detailed reply because Brünner was barking out another question:

'How is it, Monsieur, that you haven't been shot yet?'

'I . . .'

'You are responsible for everything that goes on here, aren't you?'

'That is correct,' said Kohn, aware that he was being led into a trap.

'And yet there have been a number of escapes from here, isn't that right?'

'But . . .'

'Let me make one thing clear: it is your responsibility to ensure that there are no more escapes from this hospital.'

Brünner would return periodically to the hospital in order to repeat his grim warnings. He took great pleasure in making Kohn's life as miserable as possible. A bizarre kind of relationship began to develop in which Brünner was always particularly rude and abrupt, addressing the Rothschild chief as Kohn, instead of Mr Kohn. Or he would use 'Du,' the informal manner of address in German, intending to offend. In this aim Brünner certainly succeeded. These insults were hardly serious, given the circumstances, but they nonetheless wounded the *grand bourgeois* in Armand Kohn.

The administrator could hardly plead ignorance of Nazi ideology, for he had assiduously read the *Frankfurter Zeitung* and *Das Reich*. Now he could see those theories being put into practice in the person of Aloïs Brünner. If Kohn's recent experiences were still unable to make him abandon his original strategy, then surely nothing would. He was, in fact, capable of deluding himself to a quite extraordinary degree. Far from realizing that his position was now wholly untenable, he came to precisely the opposite conclusion. One did not abandon a task simply because new challenges had presented themselves. It was through such reasoning that Armand was able to see light when there was only darkness. He remained convinced that while his relationship with Brünner was harsh and unsatisfactory, it was the very existence of their personal relationship that would assist him should the day of reckoning ever come. Ironically, Kohn's self-deception and Brünner's callous embodiment of Nazi thinking shared a common characteristic: each had a momentum all of its own.

Brünner's dire threats of reprisals horrified Armand Kohn. His overriding task was now to prevent anyone else escaping from the hospital. As chief administrator, Kohn's duty was to protect those under his jurisdiction, and especially those Jews, mothers and children, detained in the maternity wing. The hospital would have to be made still more secure. The Director General of the Rothschild Foundation, Monsieur Dupin, would have to be informed of the changes which Kohn now had it in mind to enforce. It was thus that Armand Kohn came to send the following letter, with not the slightest doubt that what he was doing was entirely correct, honourable and, above all, the execution of his duty:

Monsieur le Directeur,

There have been a number of events taking place at the hospital to which I think your attention should be drawn. Certain malintentioned individuals are placing in jeopardy the collective position of our internees. I would therefore be much obliged if you would place before M. Delepine, Chief Inspector of the Police Surveillance team, the following proposals, and to have them in force by the next day on which visits to the Rothschild Hospital are due to take place. As soon as M. Delepine has been informed, I would be obliged if you would inform the directors of all the Hospices of your decision.

Measures designed to tighten control:

1. The parcels of all visitors will be inspected in advance, and without exception.
2. Every visitor, members of UGIF included, must enter into a special register the following particulars of their identity:
   Name of visitor:
   First names:
   Number of identity card with photograph attached thereto:
3. This card is to be presented by the visitor at every visit, ready for the inspection of the warder in charge.
   A secretary is to be appointed to assist the warder in this process.
4. The length of the visit officially is to be extended to one half of one hour because of the additional time required to fill in the relevant forms.
5. Each visitor is to be asked to produce proof of his current address if this information is not set out on the piece of identity submitted for inspection. Food coupons or stamped envelopes will suffice.

A barrier is to be set up at the entrance, through which every visitor is to pass prior to entry to the Hospital.

Each registration book is to be handed in every evening to the head of each pavilion, who will be responsible for its safe keeping.

No answers are to be given to any visitor enquiring as to the purpose of these measures. If any visitor begins to protest unduly, or refuses to produce his identity papers, then the visitor is to be asked to leave and come back the following day armed with the relevant and correct documentation.

The columns on the registration books are to be headed as follows:

Visits to Internees on . . . .

Name:

First names:

Nationality:

Date of Birth:

Place of Birth:

Number of identity card (Jewish or Aryan):

Issued by:

Date of issue:

Address on identity card:

Current address:

Name and first names of person being visited:

Yours sincerely

Armand Kohn

Days later a slightly modified version of Kohn's letter was in force. The chief administrator could not help feeling proud. Surely Brünner would have no cause to complain.

*   *   *

It took Paulette little time to gather her belongings, for the simple reason that she had few. Hers was to be no elaborate departure.

An old Citroën was waiting in the grounds of the hospital. Clutching the parcel which Lobelson had hurriedly prepared, she was instructed to sit between two large Germans, the driver and an armed guard. The car headed off from Picpus towards the *boulevards extérieurs*. As it rattled over the cobblestoned streets, Paulette became aware that her stitches had not quite healed. But it was increasing fear, not pain, that now preoccupied her.

Paulette guessed that she was being taken back to her maid's attic in the twentieth *arrondissement*, where the two men would confront her with some grim news. She knew precisely what it was: after her arrest the Brigade Spéciale had done the obvious thing and conducted a search of the premises. They had found her hidden revolver, even though it had been cleverly concealed in a drawer with a false bottom. Paulette's hysteria intensified: they were going to take her back there and shoot her with her own illegal weapon. Maybe they would make it look like suicide. The car continued, without a word spoken.

Paulette knew her way around Paris. She should have guessed it earlier. She was being taken to Les Tourelles, a camp where there were many women political prisoners. But no. As they sped past the fort of Romainville, every alternative had been exhausted. Of course! She was being taken to Drancy.

When Paulette arrived at Drancy, the camp was bracing itself for the arrival of a new and tough young commandant: SS-Hauptsturmführer Aloïs Brünner. He had concluded that the only way to accelerate the rate of deportation by train was to take personal control of the entire Drancy complex. It was now Brünner who would determine Paulette's fate.

101

8

Drancy: The Anteroom of Death

For many the internment camp of Drancy was not the anteroom of death but the very room of death itself. Some detainees, particularly the women, decided that the agony had gone on too long. It was the enforced separation from their children which proved the greatest burden. In the immediate aftermath of *La Grande Rafle*, there were more than forty suicides at Drancy: at an average rate of four per week. In broad daylight prisoners would hurl themselves from the fourth floor, landing on the cornice over the ground-floor quarters. Others slashed their wrists. Those unfortunate enough to witness these desperate acts would cry out in horror.

Once the drama had subsided, however, there was precious little pity in the offing. Rather, thinly disguised anger was the prevailing emotion. Inmates hastened to brand the suicide a coward. Besides, the death of one prospective deportee simply meant that someone else would have to be substituted. The train's proposed quota of 1,000 Jews would not suddenly be amended to take account of a particular suicide. Surely, the most sensible course of action would have been to commit suicide once the train was underway. Someone else might then have been 'saved.' Such was the macabre logic of Drancy during the summer of 1943.

Drancy was an enormous, half-finished public housing complex to the north-east of Paris. It was a most unlikely setting for a camp of internment. Its well-known clock made time seem to flow so gently, and that summer the townsfolk of Drancy appeared as ever to bask in the caress of the sun. There was nothing about the area's sleepy atmosphere that betrayed the existence of a camp of horrors. Yet the mere mention of Drancy was capable of terrifying Jewish children far more than any devilish tale drawn from the rich store of Jewish folklore.

The camp had been established two years earlier when the Judenreferat ordered that the buildings be used to hold approximately 6,000 Jews about to be seized in a Paris *rafle*. Yet Drancy had never been intended as a centre for assembling deportees. In fact, when Dannecker began to make enquiries about a suitably located prison, he had looked for somewhere near to a cemetery rather than a location such as Drancy, with its convenient railway station.

From a detainee's perspective, though, Drancy was a thoroughly French institution, with French gendarmes providing the guard throughout the occupation and the place littered with rules and regulations in French. And yet from the beginning, no single French authority wanted responsibility for the camp's administration. Admiral Bard, the Prefect of the Paris Police, was eager for the Prefect of the Seine to supply the basic necessities. Prefect Charles Magny of the Seine in turn protested that he had no funds allocated for the task and threw the problem back at Bard. While the two Prefects fought it out, conditions at Drancy deteriorated. When 4,000 Jews were arrested and taken to the camp, there were only 1,200 wooden bunk-bed frames. Forty to fifty internees were crammed into one hopelessly inadequate room. When the Prefect of the Seine finally did attempt to obtain supplies of toilet paper and straw for mattresses, he was informed that it would be at least a month before materials would begin to arrive. Before long, conditions at Drancy had become a major public scandal.

The diet was a soup composed of cabbage supplied by the local markets, with virtually no nutritional value. Internees were soon afflicted with lice and skin disease. Inside, vermin roamed freely. At night, screams could be heard reverberating around the walls of the buildings. Dysentery and diarrhoea were common. Many of the more fragile internees began to succumb to the strain. The following extract from a letter written by a woman detainee to her daughter gives an indication of the atmosphere and conditions at Drancy:

> The misery and distress around us are beyond description. Just along the way are nine orphans from a boarding school. The regime is the regime of a military prison. Filth of a coal mine. Straw mattresses full of lice and fleas. Horrid overcrowding. Eighty-six women, six water faucets, you don't have time to wash. There are paralyzed women, women who have had breast operations and can't move their arms, pregnant women, blind women, deaf mutes, women on stretchers, women who have left their small children all alone. Old women of sixty-three. You can't go to the toilet more than once every sixteen hours.

Nonetheless it was everyday preoccupations that claimed the greater part of the inmates' energy. Most characteristic were the secret, almost obsessional concerns of the smoker. For many the principal and most urgent activity of the day was the feverish hunt for a cigarette. Although people still had money, many felt that their French francs would be virtually worthless after deportation. For the smoker, the most satisfactory solution was to turn cash into tobacco. The camp's extensive black market network was capable of providing almost anything. In 1943, a 'Gauloise' cost between ten and thirty francs, for Drancy prices had a habit of fluctuating wildly.

One grim economic fact was that on the eve of a deportation prices would soar. It was most prudent to buy only two or three cigarettes at a time, for no matter how much money one had, there was always the possibility of one's secret being uncovered in one of the frequent thorough searches. The most effective of all punishments took the form of the gendarme who had detected cigarettes, smoking the illicit haul in full view of the rightful owner. This was not without irony, since by far the greatest source of tobacco in the camp was the gendarmes themselves.

For the non-smoker, there were other concerns, most often to do with food: the craving for another slice of bread, a second bowl of soup, or how to obtain a smuggled slice of salami. Then there was the issue of whether a particular window should be left open or closed, or whose bed should be nearest to it. Other items much in demand were books, probably because they gave the mind a brief escape from the depression of Drancy. Racine and Balzac were always in great demand. In the men's quarters the long hours were whiled away not by lengthy discussions about the most attractive female in the adjoining block, as might have been the case in happier environs. There was an unspoken accord that it was not the right time or place for that kind of talk. Besides, there were other women on their minds: wives, mothers, sisters and fiancées. What had become of them?

The undisputed highlight of the week at Drancy was 'parcel day,' for this represented contact with the outside world: a message from a loved one; that familiar handwriting or postal mark; but above all, food. The perishables would obviously have to be consumed. What to do with the rest? Risk the black market? There was always someone ready to strike a deal. Should one indulge one's appetites immediately, or plan for next week, or next month? Everyone knew that a deportation to the East was imminent. But did that mean that one could afford to be ill-prepared upon arrival?

*　　　*　　　*

By July 2, 1943 Brünner was ready to take control of Drancy. On that day the SS man with the perpetual half-smile arrived armed with a small team of four permanent assistants, fellow Austrians belonging to the Sicherheitsdienst, the Security Service. Together they would introduce an unprecedented reign of terror and tyranny, making life at the camp still more intolerable. Brünner had already decided that to carry out Eichmann's brief properly, full and effective personal control of Drancy was essential. The entire French administration was relieved of its functions. Only the gendarmerie were accorded continued trust in being allowed to guard the exterior of the camp and to retain the right to escort deportees to the trains.

Terminology was important and Brünner immediately revised the official status of the camp. Whereas, before his arrival, Drancy was merely an 'internment camp,' from July 2 onwards it was designated an *Abwanderungslager* – a 'deportation' or 'emigration' camp. But Brünner's overriding goal was the deportation of Drancy's detainees, and his means of achieving it were far more sophisticated than his hasty revision of the camp's status. Shortly after his arrival, he initiated major reforms and refurbishments. Grubby ceilings were given a coat of bright white paint; walls and stairwells were made more presentable. Roofers, tilers, decorators and bricklayers worked night and day to make the place more fit for human habitation. The uncomfortable wooden bunks were replaced by beds with sturdier iron frames. Brooms, buckets and bins were distributed extensively. Overall, conditions soon became much more hygienic. Most welcome of all was word that food rations were to be more abundant and varied.

The main entrance to the buildings, long since smothered with barbed wire, was replaced by a large, elegant gate. Convinced that his stay at Drancy would be longer than his five-month posting to Salonika, Brünner gave orders for the construction of a plush office for his exclusive use, where he would be able to conduct his brutal interrogations. Should this task become tedious or tiring, there was a new, private shower room a stone's throw away.

Had Brünner's brief stay in France produced a change in his attitude towards the Jews? Certainly not. If anything, his hatred of the Jews had increased to the extent that he now affected physical repugnance. That was why he tried never to forget his large, black leather gloves, no matter how hot it was. Besides demonstrating that he belonged to the officer class, the gloves prevented the abhorred physical contact with a Jew. Yet every now and then Brünner would catch himself short. Gloveless, he once found himself quite unable to resist slapping the face of a passing internee. It was too late: he had dirtied his bare hands on the skin of a Jew. Disgusted with himself, the Hauptsturmführer paused for a few moments before continuing on his way, the tainted hand held limply at the waist, pointing outwards, away from the rest of his small sadistic frame. Moments later Brünner was seen wiping the offending hand against the first available wall. Nor was verbal abuse ever far from his lips, his two preferred insults being 'Jew-pig' or 'Jew-bastard.'

So Brünner's 'reforms' were never designed to improve life for the Jews. They were introduced to help him dispose of them more effectively: cattle being prepared for market. In fact, the changes for which he was responsible were introduced in an atmosphere of the utmost cynicism and tyranny. Before his programme of reconstruction, for example, the question of the submission of tenders did not arise. Brünner's technique cut out all bureaucracy:

'Who is the best-known Jewish architect in the whole of Paris?' he demanded.

Everyone knew the answer. It was Fernand Bloch.

'Where is he?'

'At his home, no doubt,' replied a trusted interpreter.

'Send someone to arrest him right away. I'm going to have him brought here. He can work under my protection.'

Those who carried out repairs to the complex did so knowing that for as long as their work continued the chances were that they would not be selected for the next convoy.

Brünner wasted no time in introducing a method of control that had been proved elsewhere. Selected detainees were to be appointed as camp officials, of sorts, and it would be they who would assist in the smooth running of Drancy. Who better to supervise and intern the Jews than the Jews themselves? It was a notion deeply familiar to Nazi ideology. Free to come and go as they pleased, these people were allowed to leave the confines of the camp in order to carry out various tasks assigned to them by Brünner. In reality, they were not free at all: they were hostages who knew very well that their failure to return was a cast-iron guarantee that any family member who remained at Drancy would automatically be executed.

This human deposit system ensured the return of this peculiar new brand of trustee. The office responsible for its administration was dubbed by Brünner the 'Mission Office.' It was established within the first week of his arrival at Drancy, placing the 'missionaries,' as they came to be known, in a dilemma. Either they co-operated with Brünner in rounding up their own relatives or they would themselves be deported, and *en famille* if possible. The 'mission' consisted of leaving the camp in order to locate any family member who remained at large and bring back that person to Drancy. Full co-operation in this task was promised by Brünner's men, particularly if there was any problem at the moment of arrest.

Many detainees were staunch supporters of the system, not because they wanted to do the Germans' work for them, but because it reinforced their belief and hope that families would remain united once deported. 'Pitchipoi' was supposed by some to be a place where families would live together in harmony; a new and challenging environment. Others were less enthusiastic about rounding up relatives and friends. Neither stance offered any freedom. Certainly no one ever volunteered to be a 'missionary': detainees were simply appointed. Collaboration increased considerably, though, and as it did so, divisions and disputes between detainees, always lurking beneath the surface, became pronounced.

'Parcel day,' previously the source of much excitement and hope, soon became a thing of the past. The new head of the camp had decreed that all parcels and correspondence be immediately suspended. There was already far too much contact with the outside world for Brünner, who was convinced that many prisoners were regular listeners to the BBC World Service, long since banned by the occupying authorities. His staff were instructed to conduct searches that would now be all the more thorough. Within weeks, Brünner's control had become a suffocating grip that left even less freedom.

*   *   *

Paulette Szlifke was not among those who shared Brünner's enthusiasm for what he called 'reuniting families.' Indeed, she had spent a substantial part of the last few months stubbornly refusing to disclose any detail whatsoever concerning the whereabouts of her parents. Not that she had abandoned hope of seeing her parents again. On the contrary, she longed to tell of her experiences at the Prefecture and the hospital. Paulette had reason to believe that her parents had been taken in by a non-Jewish family at Lausère, in the Vallée de Chevreuse, where they remained in hiding, together with an aunt.

When Aloïs Brünner took charge of Drancy, Paulette had been there about six weeks. Despite the appalling conditions, the first few days were among the happiest of her life. The reason was quite simple: she was no longer alone. As soon as she had walked into the camp she had met with close friends from Solidarité. Everyone was at Drancy: the two other members of her 'triangle,' people like herself who had been betrayed by Lucienne Kornberg, co-workers, colleagues and friends.

Although happy to see Paulette, her friends did not disguise their curiosity about the package to which she clung so tightly. It was the parcel Dr Lobelson had prepared for her. A feast awaited: chocolates, biscuits, sweets and cigarettes. Of all the new recruits to Drancy, Paulette was definitely the most welcome.

It was a week before her ebullience began to subside and she understood the purpose of the camp. People were being prepared for deportation; for a journey to the East. But exactly where, and why? No one seemed to know. It was fruitless to speculate. There were more urgent matters to attend to, one of which was not to let the more elderly folk become stripped of all hope. Paulette joined in the work of members of her group, helping the more vulnerable detainees fight off depression and despair. The youngsters would talk to those who appeared to be most downhearted, encouraging them to sing, and even staging the occasional show.

Life in the women's quarters was far removed from Paulette's world of plotting, planning and politics. Now there were more mundane matters to which she had to attend. She launched herself into the manufacture of brassières from scraps of material. She had acquired limited sewing skills from watching her father in his workshop. A woman in the same room was a corset-maker by profession and the two detainees began to work closely together, stitching away while sitting on their beds, providing underclothes for those in need. There would be a price to pay for these though: an extra slice of bread; an additional bowl of soup.

Everyone in Drancy was merely in transit, wasting away the summer hours while long lists of strange-sounding names were being drawn up in Brünner's office only a few hundred yards away. When was Paulette scheduled for deportation?

It was not just the elderly who had been suffering at Drancy. There were hundreds of children too. On arriving at their strange new home they had been bundled into bare rooms in large groups. Buckets were placed on the landings, because many of the youngest were unable to walk down the long stairways to the toilets. Unable to relieve themselves alone, they would wait uncomfortably, attempting to fight off the call of nature, hoping that help from a volunteer or an older child would not be too long in coming.

Nor had Drancy's earlier diet of cabbage soup suited the children's delicate digestive systems. Before long they were all suffering from acute diarrhoea. They soiled their clothing; they soiled the mattresses on which they spent day and night; everything became soiled. As there was no soap, the dirty underclothing was rinsed in cold water, while the child, almost naked, was instructed to wait for his underclothes to dry. A few hours later the inevitable would happen and the whole process would have to be repeated.

Very often the young ones were entirely ignorant of their own names. Any information that became available was hastily transcribed onto small wooden dog-tags. Seldom did a night pass without the constant crying of desperate children echoing all around the camp. When at last sleep came, the children often snuggled up to one another, little boys of three placing a caring arm around the smaller ones.

If one child woke up crying, the rest would do likewise and join in the chorus. When that happened, toilet troubles were certain to recur. Since there were no chamber pots for the children to use at night, and they were not allowed to venture out of their dormitories, biscuit tins were distributed in the hope that a rudimentary container was better than none at all. But few of the children dared use them, finding it virtually impossible to sit on the sharp edges without becoming badly cut.

During the day the older children would sidle up to the adults and listen to their talk about the mysterious place for which many of their relatives and friends had already set out; a place spoken about with a mixture of fear and hope. At least they could dream of finding the people they loved in this unfamiliar territory for which they too seemed bound. Could the conditions of 'Pitchipoi' be any worse than those of Drancy?

*   *   *

In Paulette Szlifke, the spirit of resistance was not easily suppressed. The plight of the inmates of Drancy only stoked up her fury and defiance. While her group led what resistance there was within the camp, there was, in fact, precious little that could be done. The game was over; they were all in captivity. Nonetheless, Paulette did smuggle out letters informing Solidarité that a transportation was being prepared, and requesting provisions for the transportees on their journey. As things were, they had few possessions; only the clothing in which they had been arrested. Solidarité responded by smuggling in sweaters and clothing more appropriate for the harsher climate of the East. Some money was also provided – not much, but enough to ensure that they would not be destitute on arrival.

Sorrowfully, Paulette recalled the summer of 1941 when, aged just seventeen, she had travelled to Drancy with a group of friends to protest against the arrests and round-ups of Parisian Jews. Then the boards and banners had read: 'Don't lose heart – the Resistance is with you!' and 'Keep your Spirits up!'

The message had been loud and clear: anything to let those detained know that there were people on the outside who were prepared to risk the might of the Reich. And then there would be the customary flight, angry *flics* giving chase and the young

111

Resistants dispersing in all directions. For Paulette that was the true spirit of dissent, with its accompanying exhilaration and fear. Now, two years later, she was herself an inmate, with no one on the outside rallying support. Furthermore, she was aware that a long and apparently arduous journey across eastern Europe was being scheduled for as early as possible.

Brünner's priority remained constant: there were to be no more delays in the programme of deportation. Not one convoy had set off since March. It was outrageous. Subordinates were always ready with explanations: twenty-one German divisions had been fighting at Stalingrad, where the Russians had taken more than 90,000 prisoners; trains, coal and fuel, the raw materials of deportation, were all in short supply.

Brünner would have none of these excuses. He was so anxious to ensure that the trains should roll again, that he had actually gone to Drancy on June 18, 1943, a fortnight before he was due to officially assume control, in order to get things moving. On that day he had seated himself behind a small table in the forecourt of the camp, with Inspector Kospereich stationed next to him, and had begun four consecutive days of interrogation of all the detainees.

Eventually, it was Paulette's turn. Their meeting was to last for less than a minute.

'Where are your parents?' demanded the Hauptsturmführer sharply.

'I have none. I'm an orphan,' replied Paulette.

She had no desire to have her family reunited by the SS.

'What about a husband, or a fiancé maybe?'

'No. I have neither. I'm only nineteen.'

Brünner moved on to the next person, and as Paulette walked away she could hear an almost identical line of questioning. It was hardly an interrogation at all, she reflected; not a patch on Commissaire David.

To Paulette it may have seemed a casual exchange, but she had evidently failed to comprehend its significance. In truth, for terror and cruelty, 'David le Rouge' lagged far behind Brünner.

Silently, and unbeknown to Paulette, Brünner had made an entry alongside her name, on the long list in front of him. During those sixty seconds he had decided upon her fate: she was to be deported immediately; to become part of his very first convoy from France. This was to depart on the morning of June 23. It was the earliest departure he had been able to arrange. It had been Brünner's intention to deport 1,000 people in that convoy; a nice round figure, easy for him, easy for the books. Yet somehow the number had crept up to 1,002.

Brünner regretted it, but there were two more who had had to be fitted in at the last moment. Paulette did not know it, but 381 French, many of them naturalized, 245 Poles, 67 Russians, 36 Dutch, 24 Greeks, 16 Belgians, 13 Czechs and more than 200 people of undetermined, but almost certainly Polish, origin, were all booked in to be part of that same convoy. One hundred and sixty of these newly designated travellers were children under the age of eighteen. The Meister der Schutzpolizei, Richard Urban, was appointed to supervise the convoy, with twenty men to assist him.

Although in France for less than two weeks, Brünner had nonetheless assumed control of the Drancy camp, organized his first convoy and apparently brought to an abrupt end France's reputation as the country most sluggish in implementing the 'Final Solution.' After Salonika, Brünner was excelling himself yet again.

There was still a good deal of work to be done before the convoy could leave. Deportees were not allowed to take money with them, and in the forty-eight hours before departure each prospective deportee was obliged to pass through the Chancellery, to exchange his or her money for a receipt. Printed only in German, the receipt specified how many francs had been deposited and pledged that the 'relevant authority' would reimburse the equivalent amount in zlotys upon arrival. Paulette handed over the money Solidarité had given her, as well as the few francs she had earned in the camp by selling brassières. Taking care not to damage her receipt, Paulette was aware that that document, incomprehensible as it was, represented her entire wealth. Still, it was reassuring to have something in writing.

Next came the search, which was usually conducted in a small shed. Paulette's passed without incident for the simple reason that there was very little to examine. The children were also searched. Toddlers of two or three entered with their minute bundles, which were carefully checked before being handed back undone. On one occasion a ten-year-old girl emerged from the shed with a bleeding ear. An inspector had torn off her earring when, in her terror, she had fumbled with the clasp. Nervously, the children would ask the adults which of their belongings they were likely to be able to keep: pictures of their parents that their mothers had given to them as they parted, with tender inscriptions hastily inscribed; medallions; little bracelets – all souvenirs of happier days.

No one knew precisely which items were likely to survive the search, for logic was alien to Drancy. One child, though, seemed able to anticipate what was in store. His mother had sewn a couple of thousand-franc notes into the lining of his clothing. Before being searched, the little boy decided on a rehearsal. Summoning a friend, he bellowed out:

'You play the policeman and see if you can find my money.'

The two children launched themselves into their impromptu deportation game.

*   *   *

The morning of June 23 had come. For many it was a relief that the waiting and wondering were at an end. Others were not so sure. At five o'clock that morning Paulette and her friends were instructed to leave their quarters. Convoy 55 was preparing to leave. With hundreds of other bleary-eyed inmates, she went down to the barbed-wire enclosure in the middle of the courtyard. Here, despite the early hour, the first thing to draw everyone's attention was a lengthy queue of men waiting to be shorn of their hair. At a long table, by the light of a hurricane lamp, the names of the prisoners were being called out briskly, with each person going to the south gate as soon as his or her name came up. Before long, the inevitable: 'Szlifke, Paulette.' Those who had not been selected were not slow to supply warm encouragement: 'Come on. Don't worry now. It's not going to be for all that long.'

Others urged: 'You keep going now, OK, because within three months from now it'll be we who are guarding the gates of Drancy.'

Most, though, seemed resigned to their lot. The fighting spirit, if it had ever existed, was not much in evidence that morning. For some months they had all been captives and now little energy remained. The words of some were hardly a farewell at all: 'All right, so you're being taken today. But next time round it'll be us – you can be sure of that.'

Paulette walked towards the familiar green-and-white city buses still serving Paris. Each was bearing the box-car number of a train. The prisoners were to be driven to Bobigny station, only a few minutes away.

The children, as ever, were ready and waiting. Always in a hurry, they would trot along, sniffling, simple little toys in their hands. Controlling them, especially at this sad dawn hour, proved very difficult. Wandering off in all directions, they would stand still for a while, only to retrace their steps. The tender but firm hand of an adult was usually there to guide them. The right road, though, was towards the railway station. However, there was a slight delay: the train would now be leaving at ten that morning.

Heavy-hearted and bitter resignation prevailed. Paulette's only remaining comfort was that she was staying with her friends. The protests and cries of indignation were kept to a minimum. In the circumstances, Convoy 55 was proceeding in an orderly fashion, just as Brünner had planned. After many months of suffering, most internees lacked the strength or inclination to stage a spontaneous revolt. One woman, realizing that her husband had been selected for Convoy 55, simply took leave of her senses, crying out and weeping hysterically. With fifty people crammed into each box-car, Paulette's overriding desire was to remain close to her friends and in this at least she was successful. The doors were sealed.

Aloïs Brünner's first convoy of French Jews began slowly to pull out of Bobigny station. He had indicated that he would be unable to attend the departure. He could not spare the time, for the preparations for the next convoy were far from complete.

Convoy 55 was on the move, shaking its way eastwards towards the Vosges. Paulette remained calm. Into some mouths went a little food, titbits brought by those who had anticipated that this journey would be their most rigorous ordeal yet. From other mouths came murmurs of ancient Hebrew prayers, full of hope that the Almighty now was there, ready to see them through this hour. A minority chose to sing; never would their spirits be crushed. Some looked on bemused, sobbing from time to time, bewildered that others still found it possible to express themselves in song.

Within a few hours of leaving Bobigny, the two pitchers of water had been emptied. Everywhere urgent pleas for water could be heard, some in French, others in German. Was anyone out there listening? Where were those in charge? The convoy continued on its journey, its large toilet-bucket filling as rapidly as the two pitchers had been emptied and exuding a nauseating odour that caused the inmates to vomit in every corner of the cattle-car. Women soon abandoned all modesty, meeting their most intimate needs with apparent naturalness. And all around was the beauty of rural France, all the more glorious now beneath the summer sun.

The freight cars of Convoy 55 contained several families, and two large families in particular. Djohar Benguigui was heading towards an unknown destination, together with her seven children: Mairie, aged eighteen, Hélène, fifteen, Adolphe, twelve, Yvonne, ten, André, seven, Hugette, four, and Jacqueline, two. In another wagon Fanny Friedmann was to be found, huddled together with her six children. Altogether Convoy 55 was transporting to the East a total of thirteen babies. As the more mobile infants crawled over the wooden planks of the freight car, their complete innocence brought tears of delight and pleasure to some, tears of despair and pain to others. Everywhere there was crying, screaming, shouting. What about some air? Some air! People were battling hard merely to breathe and grew desperate to get out of the wretched wagon.

Some of Paulette's group began urgent consultations, gathering together in small numbers, planning their escape. Paulette knew that she would not be party to it, whatever the outcome of their deliberations. Still not fully recovered from her ordeal at the hospital, she would every now and then feel the tug of a stitch. For her colleagues, though, the spirit of resistance revived itself momentarily. But as they had no tools and the struts of the floor were fixed firmly in place, escaping was easier said than done. In any case, not everyone shared their optimism, and dissent and disagreement soon broke out. It was all very well for the youngsters, the more elderly argued, but what about the reprisals that would be exacted on those left behind?

In fact the discussion was academic. Not a single soul would escape from Paulette's wagon. It had been made too secure; Brünner had seen to that. By definition, Convoy 55 was not the first to have been organized. The entire operation had been tried and tested many times before. And yet a few carriages along from Paulette's, developments had been taking place. Forty miles outside of Épernay, at one o'clock in the afternoon, the stifling heat had persuaded a guard to open the doors of the wagon. Just a little to let in some air, but enough to enable three people to make a daring jump. The following letter, written in pencil and thrown from one of the cars, reveals what it was like on the train:

> In the boxcar, on the way to Metz.
> Dear friends, last night we slept a hundred to a room in Drancy, where we were placed after the search. Some of the people were transported by stretcher. All pell-mell, sleeping on the floor . . . we are fifty to a cattle-car, sitting on the floor on our baggage. It is impossible to move. Three people escaped by jumping from a train moving at 40 or 50 mph. We don't know if they are safe. They tell us we are heading towards Metz, where there will be a selection . . . I am strong in spite of the terrible heat, without any facilities or water.

Convoy 55 was making good progress. The French officers who had accompanied the departing train handed over control at the German border. With the train now in Germany, the SS assumed full responsibility for its arrival at its destination. No more escapes now.

Stories of atrocities had filtered through to Drancy every now and then. People had begun to whisper, rumours grew and became increasingly distorted as one person passed on a confused message to the next. From the beginning, though, these stories were believed by few within the camp. And there were good economic reasons to bolster that disbelief. For by 1943 France had become the largest foreign supplier to the Reich of labour, food stuffs, raw materials and manufactured items. The system of collaboration had its own logic, and stories of atrocities simply did not fit. Everyone knew that manpower was needed in the East and all the more so now that the Germans were losing ground. France too had its own system of obligatory labour. Therefore the notion of transporting families to the East for resettlement continued to ring true for some. Paulette Szlifke certainly believed the official version of events as she settled down for her third night on the train.

At last, after three days and three nights, they arrived. More than one person had died in Paulette's wagon and several had taken leave of their senses. Yet the nightmare now appeared to have run its course. As the sides of the cattle-car were opened, Paulette headed towards her bag. There was shouting, and the barking of dogs, in the background, but Paulette's mind was preoccupied with matters financial. She was extremely anxious not to lose the receipt for her French francs. With the horrendous journey seemingly at an end, she needed that piece of paper. Feverishly, she fumbled in and around her bag.

Paulette hesitated. Had she misunderstood? No, the message was quite clear: German guards were ordering them not to bother with the bags at all; to leave absolutely everything on the train; and to hurry up about it. Surely not. Yet even the dogs seemed to be barking out that same message.

9

The Last Convoy

Armand Kohn's letter had been making an impact. Nothing dramatic to begin with, but slowly order was being restored. Kohn had battled hard to delay introducing the restrictions that were now being felt at the Rothschild Hospital. Silently and repeatedly, he ran through the chain of events that had finally persuaded him to move so decisively. Constantly he reminded himself that his first duty was to safeguard the interests of as many of his patient-detainees as possible. After each of Brünner's many visits, no one was in any doubt about the scale and nature of the reprisals that would follow should anyone else escape. Kohn had been left with no alternative but to act.

The effect of the restrictions had been almost immediate, for escapes had become few and far between. Ever the meticulous administrator, Kohn prided himself on a job well done. With each day's work complete, he would be driven home shortly before the curfew began, across the cobbled streets of Paris and towards his sumptuous apartment in the rue d'Andigne. It was during these journeys that he would reflect upon his delicate role. Obliged every day to walk a moral tight-rope, Kohn felt he was succeeding in keeping his balance and holding his head high.

Brünner was intent upon deporting patients from the hospital with or without the anguished interventions of Kohn. The Hauptsturmführer persisted in his one obsession: at least one train, once a month, with 1,000 deportees on board. And if, from time to time, there were insufficient people at Drancy to fulfil that arbitrary requirement, then others would have to be found elsewhere. If that meant throwing in some Turks or Hungarians, or others whose pedigree was not to Brünner's taste, then so be it. As long as the

119

figures added up. And if the Turks and Hungarians were lucky enough to avoid deportation, albeit temporarily, Brünner would not hesitate to visit an orphanage run by UGIF, or the old people's home attached to the Rothschild Hospital. Just as it had in the days of Dannecker, the hospital was obliged to take its turn. The quotas were the quotas; to amend them was unthinkable.

For the moment, though, the patients could breathe more easily. The reason was that Brünner was off, heading south. On September 10, 1943, he left Paris for Nice. Some thought that the main purpose of this visit was to take a break from the sordid business of deportation. In fact, Brünner was heading south not to get away from the Jews, but to do precisely the opposite. The collapse of Mussolini and the evacuation of the Italian zone presented an ideal opportunity to round up still more Jews. Never again would Brünner have to struggle to make up his numbers.

Aware that the round-ups carried out by the Italian authorities had always been half-hearted, Brünner resolved to make a proper job of their poorly organized programme. For more than two months he set about terrorizing the Jews of Nice. Within forty-eight hours of his arrival the round-ups were underway. They were particularly vicious. People who had spent considerable time and money in obtaining the correct paperwork – certificates of Aryanization, of Baptism, of communion and the like – soon discovered that their efforts had been wasted. A circumcised male was automatically deemed to be Jewish, and all documentation to the contrary was at once rendered useless. Worse still, van loads of so-called 'physiognomists' prowled the streets of Nice for anyone who, according to carefully specified criteria, looked Jewish.

Brünner requisitioned the Hôtel Excelsior. Close to the station, it was an ideal spot. In rooms that had formerly accommodated tourists in great comfort, systematic torture regularly took place. But that was by no means the main aspect of the plush hotel's new role. The objective was to transfer these temporarily detained Jews to Brünner's larger and even less hospitable base of Drancy. No sooner was the hotel full of Jews, many simply snatched from the streets, than it was emptied again to make room for the next batch.

And just as the sick had been taken from the Rothschild Hospital in Paris, so the Gestapo raided the hospitals and clinics of Nice, removing ailing and dying Jews from their beds. It did not take long for Brünner to organize in Nice a comprehensive network of informers, those prepared to betray their neighbours for some small monetary gain. During his brief stay in Nice, Brünner dispensed with his SS uniform, and went about his work in civilian clothes. As those who came into contact with him soon discovered, Brünner had no need of the formal attire of the SS: with or without it, he was a Nazi to the core.

*   *   *

On November 9, 1943, some eight weeks into his southern detour, Brünner rushed back to Drancy. The sharp eye of his aide, Bruckler, had averted a major disaster: he had discovered a tunnel. By the time Brünner came to inspect it, it was well over forty yards long. Starting in a basement beneath the office of the camp's Jewish director, the excavated passage ran directly under the barbed-wire perimeter and was planned to emerge in a nearby air-raid shelter. Another five yards and the tunnel would have been complete. Men had been working night and day to complete it. They had been helped by the fact that there was no shortage of building materials within the camp. It had been an extremely well organized operation: look-out teams had monitored people coming and going from the director's office; the entrance to the tunnel had been skilfully camouflaged; and there was even electric lighting in the narrow passage.

The prospect of Drancy being emptied in a single night horrified Brünner. He would have been the laughing stock of the entire SS. To deport the fourteen workers who had been caught would have been extremely lenient, for Brünner knew that deportation would have followed in any case. Clearly, lessons would have to be learned. The men were savagely beaten before being thrown into an underground cell. The pain of the beatings was the easiest to endure. More punishing was being forced to fill in the tunnel they had laboured so hard to create. For good measure, the entrance was cemented up. Within hours the tunnel was gone and with it a beacon of hope.

Days later the fourteen men were deported from Drancy, along with sixty-seven other camp 'leaders,' the camp's Jewish director and chief interpreter among them. Brünner had every reason to be pleased with the outcome of the tunnel affair, for it had served to further strengthen his authority. Nor did it take long for word to reach Berlin of his latest success.

Brünner's fortunes may well have been in the ascendant, but the German juggernaut of destruction was being slowed by a number of formidable barriers. Certainly there could now be no catching up with the rate of deportations from Holland. Also, there was emerging a reluctance in the French to co-operate in the arrest of Jews, which obliged the German police to rely increasingly on their own resources. With the Germans beginning to be thrust out into the open, the Jews began to submerge, often with the aid of French organizations. Prospective victims went into hiding by the tens of thousands, moving, wherever possible, across borders. This growing refusal to drift blindly towards deportation is illustrated by an incident reported by a sergeant of the Order Police whose job it was to guard a train taking deportees to the East. At Léroville nineteen Jews had jumped off the train during the night. As if to plead mitigation of his negligence, the sergeant pointed out that fourteen of these Jews were those who had tried to tunnel their way out of Drancy. This time their escape had been successful.

The increasing recalcitrance of the French administration led to a joint decision by Brünner and Knochen to employ all the available forces of the Security Police. There was to be a final, all-out drive against those Jews who remained at large.

At the same time the work of the Gestapo in France was becoming increasingly innovative. The techniques employed to make victims talk were particularly savage. Prisoners were forced to kneel on a triangular bench while a torturer climbed on their shoulders; they were suspended with their arms tied behind their back until they fainted; they were kicked, thrashed with knouts, or punched; when they fainted they were revived by a bucket of water flung over them. Teeth were filed, nails were torn out and burns were inflicted with cigarette stubs. On occasions a soldering-iron was used. Electric torture was also practised: a wire was attached to the ankles while a second was run over the most sensitive parts of the body. Both men and women suffered.

The soles of the feet were slashed with a razor and the victim forced to walk on salt. Pieces of cotton wool soaked in petrol were placed between the toes and fingers and lit. Often, the form of the torture was determined by the creativity of the interrogator, but one commonly used technique was that of the bath-tub. The 'patient' was plunged into a bath of icy water, his hands secured behind his back, and his head held under almost to the point of drowning. He would then be dragged to the surface by the hair and, if he still refused to co-operate, he would immediately be submerged again.

Brünner's new order was signed on April 14, 1944. All Jews of French nationality, save only those who were living in mixed marriages, were to be seized. To get at these troublesome Jews in hiding, rewards were to be paid to Frenchmen and women who revealed hideouts or brought in their victims. The reward was to be higher in the city than in the country, and there was some local variation in rates. Payments were to be made only after seizure. The system was characteristic of the SS: payments were to be made from the effects of the arrested Jews themselves, so that there was no additional expense to the Reich. Guarding the prisoners and transporting them to Drancy was to be carried out with the utmost care, the order specified, because in the past many transports arriving at Drancy had lost one or two passengers en route. Brünner recommended that the Jews now be roped together.

Mass round-ups like *La Grande Rafle* had become impossible: the Germans had instead to make sporadic raids on a series of arbitrary targets, ranging from labour camps to prisons and old people's homes. Early one April morning in 1944, Security Police, acting on the orders of Klaus Barbie, the head of the Lyons Gestapo, forced their way into the Colonie des Enfants, a children's home at Eyzieux. Fifty-one people were arrested: five women and forty-one children aged between three and thirteen. According to an official report, no cash or valuables were seized. Clearly, the new regulations were not being adhered to. The deportation of the children took place just one week after their arrest. But during that brief interlude, eleven-year-old Liliane Gerenstein managed to write this brief letter:

> God? How good You are, how kind, and if one had to count the number of goodnesses and kindnesses You have done us, one would never finish. God? It is You who command. It is You who are justice, it is You who reward the good and punish the evil. God? It is thanks to You that I had a beautiful life before, that I was spoiled, that I had lovely things that others do not have. God? After that, I ask You one thing only: MAKE MY PARENTS COME BACK MY POOR PARENTS PROTECT THEM (even more than You protect me) SO THAT I CAN SEE THEM AGAIN AS SOON AS POSSIBLE. MAKE THEM COME BACK AGAIN. Ah! I had such a good mother and such a good father! I have such faith in You that I thank You in advance.

Germany was losing the war. Hitler had been wrong: the 'Thousand-Year Reich' was now struggling to last slightly over ten. The Allied invasion of France, planned to deal the Nazi regime a fatal blow, took place just before dawn on June 6, 1944. Two hundred thousand men, mainly British and American, were engaged in naval operations and more than 14,000 air sorties were flown. There were some 200 aircraft per division, and neither the German air force nor the notorious U-boats were able to interfere. By the evening, 156,000 men were ashore, in the most spectacular military landing of all time.

This was the moment the Jews of France had been waiting for, for it held out the prospect of imminent salvation. But it also brought new dangers: the Gestapo, aware that time was running out, began to run amuck, carrying out mass executions and random murders; a pattern of killing-in-retreat so familiar to the Germans. With the Red Army now attacking Germany from the east, and British and American forces advancing from the west, Hitler's fate was all but sealed. Nonetheless, Berlin's orders remained the same: though beaten and in retreat, the Germans were to intensify their programme of deportations. At least the war against the Jews could be won.

In Paris the Rothschild Home for the Aged came under renewed attack; orphanages, too. Yet, finally, the tide had turned. Since the French railways were being bombed to a standstill, the deportations would surely have to stop. But Aloïs Brünner was not to be deterred so easily. Until he received specific instructions from Eichmann to do otherwise, the deportations were to continue. Aware that there remained only limited time, he had all the more reason to use it constructively. Before long, Brünner had seized on a new idea.

*   *   *

At eight o'clock in the evening of July 17, 1944, Armand Kohn made the most important telephone call of his life. He was with his mother at her private residence in the Avenue Hoche when he called his own home.

'Hello, Philippe?'

'Yes.'

'Listen to me: whatever you do, you're to stay just where you are. We're at Grandmother's. We've been arrested. The Germans are here with us now, but we are all going to stay together. Tell your sisters not to panic; everything is going to be all right, I promise you. It'll just take a few days to sort out. So just wait there for us. We'll be along right away.'

The Kohns' apartment was not far away. As Armand headed home, courtesy of the SS, Philippe, eldest of the four children, had assumed the role of head of house, albeit temporarily. Marching from one bedroom to another, he summoned his sisters and younger brother Georges-André, the latter at that moment pre-occupied with getting his cherished electric train back onto its tracks.

125

'Father has just rung. He's with Grandmother at the Avenue Hoche. The Germans are with them. And they're coming here. We're being arrested. Father says that everything is going to be all right. All that is likely to happen is that we'll be taken away for a few days. Then we'll come home again and everything will be all right. In any case, the war's almost over now, so they won't be able to keep us all that long.'

The hand of Brünner was not difficult to detect. All along it had been his intention to deport the head of the Rothschild Hospital. The only issue over which there had been any element of doubt was that of timing. Now the time was right. While Kohn was aware that his relations with Brünner were undeniably strained, he had nonetheless always assumed that that relationship, however unsatisfactory and hard to endure, would one day protect him. That day of reckoning had now come, yet Kohn evidently had no understanding of how the SS chief's mind worked.

Brünner's technique was well tested. He simply accused Kohn of having organized systematic sabotage at the hospital. On this slender evidence compounded of whim and fantasy, Kohn was being arrested along with the six other members of his family. Even though his own safety was now under threat, he did not, even momentarily, consider urging his family to escape while the opportunity remained. On the contrary, he went out of his way to advise them to stay where they were and to prepare for departure.

Within half an hour, a bus had pulled up outside 2 rue d'Andigne. As Kohn walked into his apartment, accompanied by two German policemen, his children focused on their father's grim expression.

'Go and get your bags ready,' he ordered.

Silently, the children did as they had been told. Philippe had an opportunity to escape, even at this late stage, but as he contemplated the prospect of quietly disappearing by the domestic's entrance, the familiar words of his father echoed in his mind: 'Don't forget you'll have on your conscience the death of the entire family.'

Hastily, Philippe prepared to present himself for arrest. One by one the children appeared. The bus started up again. Next stop: Drancy.

Remarkably, Brünner's determination to continue with the deportations was resulting in some success. Another convoy was poised to leave Drancy, among the unwilling passengers over 300 Jewish children. Jewish children were never exempt from Brünner's programme. Now, with the French Resistance enjoying increasing success against the occupying forces, Brünner had coined a phrase for the toddlers: 'future terrorists.' Children today; terrorists tomorrow. Therefore they had to be deported. In all, more than 1,300 people were deported from Drancy on what was to be Brünner's last regular convoy: number 77. It left Drancy on July 31, 1944, and included one baby born in the camp, the tiniest future terrorist imaginable.

The Kohns were not on that convoy, although they did witness its departure from Drancy. The general acceptance that this was the last convoy gave Armand Kohn renewed hope.

'Nothing is going to happen to us. We're only going to be here for a matter of days, after which we'll all be back at home. You'll see.'

And it was true: the Kohns were better off than most at Drancy. Perhaps Armand's position counted for something after all. They would not dare deport him, for he was one of the most prominent Jews in the whole of France.

Brünner had every reason to feel satisfied with himself, despite the news of military set-backs. To have organized that final convoy was a remarkable feat. He had done as much as Eichmann had asked. He had arrived in France only in June of 1943, yet had overseen the departure of seven convoys before the end of the year. And from January 1944 until the warm summer in which he now found himself, he had been responsible for organizing a further fourteen.

The Americans were advancing rapidly, and the gates of Paris were within striking distance. The city was poised for liberation. General Leclerc's tanks were to be heard echoing to the north of the city, music to the ears of most Parisians. The 1,500 Jews still incarcerated in Drancy were likewise inspired by the distant sound of cannons and gunfire. Within days, if not hours, they would be free. Brünner paced around his office at Drancy. He realized that the evacuation of the entire complex would have to be conducted as speedily as possible, but that he too would soon be leaving France.

A knock on Armand Kohn's door. The entrant wore a serious expression.

'Mr Armand Kohn, you are to go to Brünner's office right away.'

Kohn braced himself, wondering what he could want. Perhaps it concerned the hospital. Glancing at Philippe, Armand tried to convey his familiar message that everything would be all right and that he would be back before long. Within minutes he had indeed returned. But everything was far from all right. The man who had had every opportunity to leave France, who was as patriotic as any Frenchman, who had been injured in the defence of his country, who dearly loved his family and home, but stubbornly refused to heed the advice of others, was to be deported. And every member of his family would be accompanying him. Armand braced himself and told his family what Brünner had just said.

'We're going to be leaving here. Get your bags ready. We'll all still be together.'

Philippe could not understand. Leaving for where? In any case, he had believed that the convoy containing the 300 children was the last regular convoy. In that assumption he was correct. Convoy 77 was indeed the last regular convoy; the Kohns' convoy was distinctly irregular.

As Brünner issued detailed instructions for the camp's archives to be burned, he discovered that there were no more trains available for the purpose of deportation. The forty-eight wagons which he had earmarked to deport the 1,467 Jews who remained at Drancy, had been requisitioned by the Wehrmacht for the repatriation of German soldiers. Furious, Brünner immediately called for a car to drive him to Bobigny station, to find out exactly what was going on. On the station platform an officer of the Wehrmacht towered over Brünner.

'This is my train and you know it,' protested the SS man.

'Well, now it's mine,' retorted a war-weary colonel.

'I'm sorry, but I really don't think you understand. I have a mission to fulfil; an essential mission. Stop this immediately and get your men off this train.'

Brünner was sickened by the very sight of this group of demoralized and tired soldiers.

'Well I'm acting under orders too: to fight a war and get my soldiers back home, with as many wounded and as much material as possible,' parried the army man.

'You'll be aware that in my capacity as an SS officer my orders are to receive priority over yours. I have to deport some 1,500 Jews.'

The colonel paused momentarily, wondering if he had understood what the little man had just said.

'Deport some Jews! I couldn't give a damn. Do you honestly think that it's better to deport 1,500 Jews than repatriate 1,500 German soldiers? Do you think that a lousy 1,500 Jews are going to help Germany win the war?'

'This train belongs to me and you'll not have it,' retorted the stubborn SS-Hauptsturmführer.

'Well take it from me. If you can. And you can stick your bloody Jews.'

It was not the moment to determine who had more right to the train. Besides, with more than 1,000 weary German troops already on board, Brünner was hardly in a strong position to negotiate. Still, he could be as pragmatic as the next man. Aware that most German soldiers were desperately hungry, particularly for meat, he used the supplies of food at Drancy to his advantage. Soon he had struck a most unorthodox deal. He had succeeded in obtaining three carriages from an aircraft battery, in exchange for two pigs, a cage of chickens, some geese and some red wine with which the soldiers would be able to wash down their unexpected feast. Brünner was to have the last three wagons of train number 1697: one for the Gestapo, one for the *Grüne Polizei*, the green-uniformed German police who had been stationed in France, and most importantly of all, one for his precious deportees. The carriages were to be attached to three more containing cannons and other weaponry. Brünner calculated that he would be able to squeeze in just over fifty Jews. He had no difficulty in deciding who seven of those were to be: the Kohns. All along, Brünner had been waiting for an opportunity to deport Kohn and his family. Now, finally, on the eve of the liberation of Paris, that moment had come.

On Thursday August 17, 1944, the sun shone brightly during the afternoon. For Brünner and Kohn alike, the days of Drancy were coming to a close. The last details for evacuation had been agreed.

The two sisters, Antoinette and Rose-Marie, were the first of the Kohns to clamber into the cattle-car. At least thirty men were already sprawled around the narrow confines of the wagon. The sudden arrival of two young women in colourful floral dresses caused a considerable stir. Armand Kohn helped his wife onto the train. Georges-André, lighter and smaller than the rest, was the easiest to install, in an almost effortless airlift. Finally, it was the turn of Armand's mother, Marie-Jeanne. The old lady at first refused:

'How on earth do you expect me to get on? There aren't even any steps.'

Armand knew that if he failed to act decisively, his family would be the laughing stock of the entire car. He would not be made to look a fool. There stood his mother, a yard or two away, periodically standing on her toes in order to indicate that the prospect of her climbing onto the train was extremely remote. One well-built man could not bear to watch the small drama unfold any further. He leapt down and hoisted the old lady into the cattle-car. She uttered not a word of protest. Armand knew that her sudden silence was a time-honoured ploy to disguise a seething rage. Beside herself with fury, Marie-Jeanne Kohn's hands shook with humiliation.

Next on board was a policeman. He was there to conduct a search for weapons, valuables and anything on a long list of forbidden items. A few months earlier he would not have hesitated in disposing of the cases stacked in a corner. Now, there was simply not the time and instead he satisfied himself with the briefest of inspections. But even that produced a more than satisfactory yield, and soon his pockets overflowed with chocolates and cigarettes.

Armand Kohn took a closer look at the men with whom he was sharing the cattle-car. They were a rough bunch. Many had been transferred from the prison at Fresnes, where they were serving sentences for having defied the authority of the Reich. At least one was under sentence of death. These Resistance fighters were from a number of different factions, an assortment of Zionists and Communists, all branded 'terrorists' by Brünner. So that there could be no misunderstanding, he had chalked onto the cattle-car, in the clearest of hands, the words 'Juden Terroristen.' Most were members of the OJC, the Organisation Juive de Combat. Also on board were some French policemen who, unusually, had been active in the Resistance, until caught or betrayed.

When these prisoners had first arrived at Drancy, after their transfer from Fresnes, Brünner had decided that there was not time to instruct those Jews who witnessed their arrival to disperse. Preferring a more direct approach, he hurled a number of hand-grenades into the air and fired wildly with the revolver which rarely left his side. Naturally, the onlookers had dispersed. The new arrivals were escorted to a prison within the prison of Drancy. Now they found themselves in a cattle-car, competing for the little space there was with the Kohn family, whose members were as far removed from the world of armed combat and Zionism as could be imagined.

There was one man, though, who appeared to belong to no particular faction. Armand paused for a moment. The face was familiar. The man opposite in the beret was Marcel Bloch, the celebrated manufacturer of aeroplanes. There were one or two others, too, who appeared to come from the ranks of the well-to-do. Unwittingly, people had edged themselves into small groups. The crammed cattle-car contained in microcosm the history and diversity of the Jews in France.

The hostile feelings of the Kohn contingency towards those

with whom they were now forced to rub shoulders were certainly reciprocated. If anything, the contempt of the Resistants for the fuller faces opposite, soon dubbed 'les bourgeois,' was even more pronounced. Within no time the train's entire combat division knew that the dark-haired, bespectacled man with the large family was Monsieur Armand Kohn, until recently head of the Rothschild Hospital and a leading light in UGIF.

UGIF! The very name made those in the Resistance shudder with disdain. In fact, there was another nickname, still less complimentary, for the likes of those who had chosen to work for that organization. Long ago its members had been classified as the *Broona Yidelach*, a derisory Yiddish term meaning 'little brown-shirted Jews.' In other words, collaborators.

At five o'clock Brünner's aide Bruckler indicated that it was time to leave. The large door of the cattle-car was slammed and secured. Brünner's last convoy pulled out of Bobigny station. It was the most unconventional deportation organized to date: a motley assortment of fleeing Gestapo members, green-uniformed policemen and a cattle-car full of Jews. Brünner was delighted: against all the odds, his improvised plan appeared to have succeeded. Leaving his trusted aide in charge, Brünner would take an alternative route home.

To begin with, progress was very slow, with frequent unexplained stops. The rumble of retreating German lorries was heard from the road that intermittently ran parallel with the long, straight railway line. Almost immediately it was agreed to share the provisions that had survived the earlier cursory search. Some of the prisoners from Fresnes had not set their eyes on such a feast for over three years. Dividing themselves into five groups of ten, the occupants of the last carriage of the last convoy lit cigarettes, broke off pieces of bread, and savoured the taste of every piece of chocolate that the inmates of Drancy had handed over to fortify their departing friends. For the Kohn family, used to having whatever they wanted when they wanted it, and usually served to them at that, such democratic sharing was alien in the extreme.

Resistants active at Drancy had done their best to supply the deportees with all the tools necessary for an escape. A number of loaves had been stuffed with a variety of equipment, including files, screwdrivers, and hammers, and there was even a small metal-saw. If the deportees could not escape, they would have only themselves to blame.

The head of the wagon had authorized work to begin as soon as the train had left. For many of the fighters, this was not their first attempt at escape: between them, they had succeeded in liberating themselves from a number of prisons. Urgently, the well-trained hands set about their task. The Resistance fighters feared that 'les bourgeois' would have no hesitation in reporting them to their SS guards. This select group evidently realized that they had a good deal less to gain from making a jump for it. Or did they? Whatever the case, they would have to be watched very closely. There was also the constant hazard of sudden inspection by the SS. The guards were at all times armed with machine guns, and the men now at work were well aware of what would happen if things did not go as planned.

Armand Kohn was not impressed by the enthusiasm for escape which now gripped the majority. It was all very well for them, but what about his mother, who did not enjoy the best of health; and what about little Georges-André? The Germans would not hesitate to carry out reprisals. He had seen it all before at the hospital. He was therefore firmly opposed to escaping. Besides, he had another idea. It was a long shot, but at least it would not put others in jeopardy. He would write a letter. As always, he was carrying five pens, each with a different-coloured ink, each for a distinct purpose. The black pen was the right one for the job. Installing himself rather precariously on a suitcase, Armand took from his leather wallet a small visiting card. He decided to use capitals, given the shaking of the train. It was a desperate plea:

17.VIII.44. DEAR SIR,

WE ARE ALL DEPORTEES. NO DOUBT WE'RE HEADING TOWARDS GERMANY, BUT WE'RE ARMED WITH COURAGE AND FAITH IN

GOD. WE'RE WITH SOME POLITICAL PRISONERS FROM FRESNES. WHY? TRY AND DO SOMETHING FOR US, VIA THE INTERNATIONAL RED CROSS. GO AND SEE THE HEAD OF THE PARIS CITY COUNCIL. FAREWELL. SEE YOU SOON. THINK OF US. WARN OUR FRIENDS, AND THOSE AT THE BUSINESS.

The message was complete. He took out a small envelope and addressed the letter to a business friend with whom he had maintained contact:

M. Robert Carré,
Secretary,
29b rue Doudeauville,
Paris XVIII

On the back of the envelope he added a final request: 'WOULD THE PERSON WHO FINDS THIS LETTER BE GOOD ENOUGH TO POST IT.' Armand Kohn even supplied a stamp; his wallet had always resembled a miniature post office. As the train sped through the town of Villers-Cotterets in Aisne, Kohn slid his polite plea through two planks on the cattle-car's floor, and it fluttered on to the track below. There could hardly have been a larger letter box. Hours later the message was picked up by a local resident who happened to be passing by and who decided on the spot to send it on.

Certainly there was nothing to lose. Yet it was ludicrous, the notion that at this late stage Kohn might still be able to count on the intervention of a prominent official from the Paris city council. Even so, others wanted a turn. Not to contact the International Red Cross, but to communicate with loved ones, relatives and friends. Here was Armand Kohn, stubborn and conservative in his ways, teaching a trick or two to hardened Resistants. However, with over a dozen people now wanting to write, they could muster only two blunt pencils between them. It was Philippe who crossed the delicate divide between the camp of 'les bourgeois' and the rougher domain of Brünner's 'Juden Terroristen,' taking with him his father's five precious pens as an initial peace offering.

Food had been eaten, letters written, factions formed and escape efforts begun. All the while the train's progress remained pitifully slow. Then came a sudden quickening of its pace and, before long, nightfall. The nocturnal rituals of the Kohns astonished the former inmates of Fresnes as, one after the other, they started to change into their night attire, each member of the family in turn using a make-shift structure like a beach hut, which Philippe and his father had ingeniously devised. The scene was a cross between comedy and farce. For the Kohns, though, it was no laughing matter: they had always cherished privacy and comfort; they were not about to abandon the habits of a lifetime merely because they now found themselves locked in a wooden box.

The following morning, the quiet whirr of Armand's battery-driven razor in time attracted everyone's attention. This meticulous, clean-shaven man, used only to the very best, still wore a white shirt and a restrained tie beneath a sober-coloured suit. It was as if he was about to set off from his apartment for another day at the office. Had he still not grasped the gravity of his plight?

In fact, Armand Kohn had finally seen his error. Yes, he had believed in his strategy of staying in Paris and in the importance of his work at the hospital. But he had been wrong. In a corner of the train belonging to no particular faction, he had perched himself on a leather suitcase. Philippe went over to comfort his father. The old man whose stubbornness no one could penetrate, had evidently got through to himself. He was in tears. Never before had he been so frank:

It's no good. I have failed. It's all over. I had intended to protect you all, and steer you through this miserable war. And now here we all are in this cattle-car going goodness-knows-where. All because of me.

Sobbing, he no longer sought to disguise his pained expression. Other members of the family rallied round, trying to comfort him. Even the young Georges-André attempted to boost his father's flagging spirits. In the end, Armand had had to confess his failure.

135

It may have been too late, yet he showed every sign of becoming a reformed man.

The Resistants opposite had begun to sing the eternal Jewish song of hope for the oppressed, the *Hatikvwah*, followed by an enthusiastic rendition of *La Marseillaise*. As the songs of hope and defiance rang through the wagon, escape-work quietly went on in one corner. In comparison with the pace of the train, progress was rapid.

By the summer of 1944 the Allies had achieved absolute superiority in the air. Long-range aircraft were reaching all parts of the Reich, bombing a wide variety of targets and paralysing Germany. Brünner's convoy, too, came under fire. The unmistakable sound of aircraft provoked unrestrained rejoicing in the last wagon. Marcel Bloch confirmed that they were Spitfires. Four of them were darting back and forth, high in the skies. The bad news was that they suddenly opened fire, strafing the convoy. The head of the wagon ordered everyone to sprawl on the floor. The train's cargo of heavy weaponry could be seen clearly, and the RAF were in no doubt that their target was legitimate. Within seconds the rear of the train had been hit, but the occupants of the last wagon were not injured. The train came slowly to a halt. Voices could be heard declaring that it was impossible to continue the journey.

Armand Kohn was delighted, for at the very least there would be a delay. With the war in Europe rapidly coming to a close, any delay was welcome. But no sooner had the Spitfires launched their attack, than they were gone. Furthermore, the voices were wrong: within hours the train was ready to press on. Another hope had been dashed.

It soon became evident that Armand Kohn had undergone only a partial reformation. A revolution in his reasoning had been too much to expect. Was there not now a point to be scored from the incident of the four Spitfires?, Kohn argued. The attack provided irrefutable evidence that the end of the war was only days away. There was considerably more risk in attempting to jump from the train than in seeing the journey through, he insisted. Brünner had given ample warning that even a single escape would automatically mean the end for everyone. Armand's message was directed towards the ears of Philippe, its tone severe and threatening:

> I absolutely forbid you to leave this train. Just think, if you do make a jump for it, you're going to have to live with the fact that you were responsible for the death of the entire family. So long as we all stay together, everything will be all right, I promise you.

Philippe Kohn, at twenty-one, was finally ready to make the break from the suffocating hold of his father. The *chef de famille* was wrong. When the opportunity presented itself, Philippe would join those escaping. Much to his astonishment, his younger sister Rose-Marie announced that she would join him. After four years in occupied Paris, four years of doing precisely as she was told, she, too, was ready to break free.

Antoinette, the elder sister, said that she would remain with her parents, to look after them on arrival. For Marie-Jeanne Kohn, in poor health even before setting foot on the train, it was clearly out of the question to jump. The young boy, Georges-André, was anxious to share the new-found independence of his elder brother. This time, though, no veto was barked out by Armand. Instead, his wife Suzanne quietly said that she would not part with the boy, insisting that he was far too young to even think of jumping from a moving train. The Kohn family itself was now divided. When the time came, two would be jumping, five staying put. Armand Kohn had been defied by two of his children, and for the first time there was absolutely nothing he could do about it.

At one o'clock on the morning of August 20, 1944, the Resistants indicated that their work was complete: there was a large hole in the cattle-car. Preparations for the escape had been meticulous: numbers were allocated, food and money distributed. Armand was standing helplessly in his pyjamas, bracing himself for a final confrontation with his son.

'For the last time, Philippe, I absolutely forbid you to leave.'

A blessing came to the young man from the most unexpected of quarters. Grandmother Kohn was searching for something to which she evidently attached a great deal of importance. It was her watch.

'You are right to go. Take this with you,' she said, handing Philippe the watch.

Aware that he was wasting his breath, Armand nonetheless could not prevent himself from rattling out the orders:

'Philippe, why don't you listen to what I'm telling you? You'll have on your conscience the death of all of us. I order you to stay.'

Philippe edged towards his mother, embracing her tenderly, wanting but not daring to ask her to join those now precariously poised to jump. It was unthinkable. Suddenly, a compromise struck him:

'I beg you, if you won't come, then just let me take Georges-André.'

Fired by Philippe's new proposal, the boy struggled to free himself from the tight embrace of his mother's arms. The answer was no. Georges-André was staying and that was the end of the matter. Philippe had no time to convince the rest of the family. If there was one thing for which his father stood above all else, it was the principle of family unity. The others had to stay.

The time had come to jump. Straddling the side of the cattle-car, Philippe hurled himself into the night air, finally free of his father. He landed with a damp thud on soft earth; it had been raining. They were still well inside France, at Morcourt, not far from St Quentin. Moments later Rose-Marie jumped, although she knew immediately that she had not made a particularly good job of it, her legs and arms spreadeagling wildly. Still, she too was free. Altogether, twenty-seven people escaped, among them a rabbi.

Three hours after the escape, Convoy 79 once again ground to a halt. It had by now grown a little lighter and the hole which had been made by the Resistance men was there, inviting inspection. The twenty or so people who remained immediately agreed: everyone had been asleep at the time. It was as great a surprise to them as it was to Bruckler, who, seething, mounted the wagon. Everyone was ordered out, the remaining members of the Kohn family clutching Armand.

'You can't say you weren't warned,' Bruckler shrieked in German, 'Every single one of you is going to be shot.'

Handing a shovel to Kohn, he commanded, 'Start digging.'

The SS executioners stood nearby as Armand Kohn was instructed to dig a grave large enough to accommodate both him and his family. He refused point-blank. For the first time in his life, Kohn had refused to do what a person in authority had ordered. Aware of the likely consequences for those who remained, he cursed Philippe and the other escapees. At the same time he wished them well.

'So long as I'm in charge here, no one is going to be shot. If anyone is to be punished, it's those who were not doing their job properly in guarding the prisoners.'

It was the voice of an officer from the Luftwaffe.

Bruckler was furious. He had been humiliated in front of a bunch of Jews. Help had come when it was least expected and from the most unlikely of quarters: the Kohn family saved by a German officer.

An hour later Bruckler was back, seeking revenge for his recent dressing-down:

'I've just heard from the Kommandantur that everyone who escaped has been captured and shot on the spot,' he announced with undisguised pleasure.

Bruckler's words had a brief impact, but it was obvious from his expression that he was lying. Yet uncertainty about the safety and well-being of his two children raged in Armand's mind. The train moved on again, this time, though, without hope for the prisoners: there was now an armed guard in the cattle-car itself.

By Friday August 25, 1944, eight days after it had set out from Bobigny, Brünner's convoy finally reached its destination: Weimar. The door of the cattle-car was flung open, Bruckler standing by and clutching Brünner's original list. Hastily, he began to amend the details in an attempt to cover up the escapes that had taken place under his nose.

As he stood on the platform of the railway station, Armand had in his wallet the *carte de légitimation* issued by UGIF. The words were quite unambiguous:

M. Armand Kohn, Administrator at the Rothschild Hospital . . . is hereby exempt from all measures of internment. This protection extends and applies to any family member living with him.

As the four remaining members of his family — mother, wife, daughter and son — prepared to go their separate ways, the process of enlightenment on which Kohn had embarked during the long journey east was finally complete. He could now see that his strategy had been a disaster. The promise was not worth the paper it was printed on; nor had it ever been. Everything seemed so clear now.

10

'Ce n'est pas une boulangerie'

For Paulette Szlifke, too, matters were considerably more clear. Thirteen months earlier she had been scrambling around the floor of a cattle-car for a piece of paper. Without that precious document, Paulette had feared that she would be left with nothing. Her fear turned out to be well founded.

In another sense, though, Paulette was fortunate. For unlike the majority of the 1,002 prisoners who had set off on Convoy 55, she was still alive. Hundreds of others had long since perished. Paulette had survived a little over a year in an obscure spot in southern Poland: Auschwitz. This was the much-heralded 'East.' This was the 'Pitchipoi' dreamed of by the children of Drancy.

Auschwitz was quite unique. A large collection of buildings had been constructed to form a vast concentration camp. This served one precise purpose: the systematic extermination of human beings. There was always room for gypsies, Communists, homosexuals, criminals and others despised by the Reich, but most of the victims were there because they were Jews. Here was Hitler's 'Final Solution' in action, for Auschwitz was journey's end for every one of the convoys despatched from France. Families had been taken there not to be reunited, but annihilated. Paulette Szlifke, still only in her teens, had been clinging precariously to life in the most lethal death camp ever devised.

The struggle to survive had begun as soon as the doors of Convoy 55 were flung open by the SS guards. Cold, tired and hungry from the journey, the weary occupants of Paulette's carriage were immediately ordered out onto the platform below. The SS meted

141

out fierce blows to those who responded too slowly. Guard dogs barked at the new arrivals. A loudspeaker instructed the prisoners to remain calm, but panic soon set in along the entire length of the train. The language may have been unfamiliar, but the message was clear: the only thing possible was to do exactly as instructed. There was hitting and shoving in all directions and orders were rattled out all around. The prisoners found themselves doing precisely the same as those in front of them, and everyone was swept along in a human tide. Many were simply relieved to abandon the stinking cattle-cars. At least there was air, and space to move again. In the chaos, several people, mainly elderly ladies, collapsed from exhaustion, only to be forced to their feet again.

Having abandoned the prospect of retrieving her receipt, Paulette was above all anxious to not be separated from her friends. What struck her most of all was the spectacle of one hundred or so prisoners, dressed in striped pyjamas, each bearing a number and a capital letter that appeared to indicate nationality. They were barely more than skeletons, their demeanour all the more pitiful on account of their shaven heads.

As Paulette shuffled around next to the train, she could come to only one sensible conclusion. Whispering to a colleague from Solidarité, she said:

'This can't be for us. We must just be passing through. It's got to be a temporary stop. We'll be moving on again in a while.'

The muffled voice next to her agreed at once:

'Yes. You must be right. God only knows, but those people look half-dead. We won't end up here. For goodness sake – we're French – we're political prisoners. We won't be here long.'

Both were right – in a way. Auschwitz had not been designed to accommodate long-term prisoners. The camp had been established only in 1940, with Rudolf Höss as commandant. Höss's brief was to open a camp capable of housing 10,000 prisoners. By the summer of 1941, however, he had been summoned to Berlin, where he was informed by Himmler that Hitler had decided on the 'Final Solution' to the Jewish problem. Auschwitz had been designated the principal site. It would therefore have to be transformed from concentration camp to extermination camp. Architects worked long hours and German firms were invited to tender for contracts to provide materials and installations.

The centrepiece of Auschwitz was its huge gas chambers and furnaces. The latter were to burn not ordinary fuels but human beings – Jews for the most part. This meticulous plan functioned extremely efficiently, with hundreds of thousands perishing month after month. True, there was the occasional problem. During August and September of 1942, for example, the convoys of Jews arriving from France were so numerous that the arrangements for killing prisoners by gas proved insufficient. The spirit of improvisation came to the rescue, for within days whole convoys of Jews were being shot instead. Yet there were the words, plain for all to see, '*Arbeit macht frei!*' – 'Work makes you free' – in large lettering in an arc above the camp's main entrance.

Paulette Szlifke was lucky to have set eyes on that sign, for many never even made it that far. A process had been formulated to determine who should die immediately and who should be worked and starved to death. The entire operation, known as 'selection,' followed strict criteria issued by Berlin and was overseen by a small group of SS doctors. They were there, ready to spring into action as the weary occupants of Convoy 55 spilled out onto the platform.

As children were snatched from the arms of their mothers, there were screams of fury and fear; husbands and wives waved to one another helplessly as they were led their separate ways – and all at the double. It seemed that everyone was being put into a particular category. Different groups were beginning to emerge: young people, old people, women with children, women without children, able-bodied men, the sick and infirm. But why? There were a few large open trucks in the distance, and a vehicle apparently bearing the sign of the International Red Cross. Their presence led some to believe that help might be to hand. Paulette noticed the older men, women and children heading towards the trucks.

Paulette's friend from Solidarité was in no doubt about the most prudent place to be:

143

'Why don't you go over there with that lot?,' she said, pointing towards one of the trucks in the distance, where people could be seen mounting a small ladder to the rear of the vehicle.

The girl from Solidarité was aware that Paulette was still recovering from her operation. Besides, one could not be too proud about these matters; the more energy one conserved, the better off one would be.

Paulette took no time to answer:

'No. I'll walk with you. I'll be all right. Now don't you start fussing about me.'

To be parted from her friends? The very notion was ludicrous. She had experienced days of isolation and was determined not to do so again. True, she was a little tender, but who was in the peak of health? Not that her decision to walk was a considered response: she had simply followed her feelings. Only some days later did Paulette come to realize that this hasty rejection of her friend's advice had, in fact, saved her life; that the trucks escorted by the car seemingly belonging to the Red Cross had made their way directly to the gas chambers. Quite unwittingly, the young rebel had survived the process of 'selection,' that arbitrary decision to preserve or dispense with human life. Relatively speaking, Paulette was fortunate to have participated in the selection process. For only a few weeks before, three convoys from Drancy had been sent straight to the gas chambers, with not a single soul spared.

Paulette's friend was not the only one to encourage another in the wrong direction. One man from Paulette's convoy became convinced that the selection process was to determine who should receive the most lenient treatment. He reasoned that this was why the young and the old were being singled out. Noticing that his fourteen-year-old son was in a line with four young men who appeared to be a good deal older, the worried father felt compelled to act. Stepping out of his own row, he made an urgent request to a nearby SS officer. He wished to have his son transferred to the other queue. Immediately, his request was granted. Only later did he realize that, innocently and with the very best of intentions, he had sentenced his son to death. As Paulette went in one direction, the young boy, along with hundreds of others, went in the other.

Paulette and her group were led into a barracks. Instructed to remove every item of clothing, the young women were within minutes naked, arms and elbows clumsily manoeuvring in an attempt to preserve some modesty. Next, an obligatory cold shower: no soap, no towels, just the briefest rinse. Still wet, the new arrivals were ordered out of the barracks. Each girl then had her hair shaved, pubic hair included. Then came the tattooing. Ordered to present her left arm, Paulette underwent a radical transformation. As far as the authorities were concerned, Paulette had ceased to exist. All that mattered now was her number. Paulette Szlifke had become 46650.

The well-fed Jewish women attending to the new arrivals warned them never to forget their number, and to know it in both German and Polish. To get one's number wrong, to fail to hear it when called out – in fact, to do anything other than recite it with precision and speed when ordered so to do – could mean paying the highest price.

Four-six-six-five-zero. Four-six-six-five-zero. Again. And again. Within minutes the number was imprinted on Paulette's mind. Of those who had arrived at Auschwitz on Convoy 55, only 217 women survived the selection process: those who had been assigned numbers 46537 to 46753. And there, somewhere among them, stood Paulette, an anonymous entity hidden almost exactly in the middle. She had earlier whispered to the woman whose job it was to remove her hair:

'What on earth is going on in this place? We're political prisoners you know . . . from France . . . and where have the others gone?'

The only response from the barber-prisoner was to mutter repeatedly 'Himmel Kommando.' Paulette failed to grasp what the woman meant. Not that she was incapable of translating the words: they simply meant 'Kommando of the Sky.' Whenever the woman whispered this nonsensical phrase, she pointed towards the large chimneys in the distance. Paulette could only conclude that the strain of concentration-camp life had taken its toll. The woman was speaking gibberish.

Shorn of their hair, stripped of their clothes, Paulette and her friends had difficulty in recognizing each other. When Paulette glimpsed a reflection of herself in a pane of glass, she struggled to even recognize herself. As night set in, and the tattooing ended, the young prisoners were unceremoniously dumped outside in the open, naked, branded and freezing. Paulette survived that first Auschwitz night, huddled next to friends to conserve the heat generated by their bodies. Others in her group did not make it.

Only in the middle of the following morning did the distribution of clothing begin. Paulette's contingent soon found themselves in the most unexpected of attire: uniforms of Russian conscripts who had been massacred at the camp. Despite their grim and recent history, Paulette could not prevent a peculiar feeling: she was proud to wear the uniform of the Red Army. With her shoes odd in both size and appearance, Paulette had little idea at that time how fortunate she was to have a pair of shoes. Unaware that the loss or theft of even one shoe could automatically signal her death, she still had many of the lessons of Auschwitz to learn.

The Nazi system of progressive dehumanization was now well advanced. All that the process needed was the passage of time. It would not take long. Stripped of her own clothing; shorn of her hair; branded like a beast; isolated from her family; insulted from all quarters; obliged to exist on a starvation diet; unable even to control her bladder; surrounded by dysentery and disease; constantly cold and vulnerable to the elements: Paulette faced destruction by Auschwitz.

The process affected not just inmates battling to retain a sense of identity, but their SS guards, too. In time – weeks for some, months for others – some prisoners began to behave like animals, fulfilling the role so carefully prepared for them. Nowhere was this more evident than at roll-call, such an important feature of life at Auschwitz.

Roll-call was a twice-daily ritual, although often there would be more. Time to leave the barracks, no matter what the weather, and

to line up according to height. Four-six-six-five-zero. Each time Paulette would silently rehearse her number. The roll-call would last at least an hour, often much longer. Its purpose was usually to ensure that everyone was accounted for, but every now and then it was also used for selecting people for the gas chambers.

It had taken some forty-eight hours from her arrival at Auschwitz for Paulette to realize precisely what the barber had been saying. The 'Himmel Kommando' was camp talk for the gas chambers. The large chimneys to which the woman had pointed and which Paulette had by now seen in operation, had a most unlikely function: the systematic burning of human beings. Slowly, Paulette's mind began to admit the truth. At Drancy she had heard rumours of atrocities, but no one had taken them seriously. Reports of widespread massacres had even been broadcast by the BBC, whose bulletins were monitored by Resistants at Drancy. But these reports had also been largely discounted. Only now, a year later, did Paulette realize that the unbelievable, the unthinkable and the unspeakable were ordinary, everyday events at Auschwitz.

For those who sought proof of atrocities, Paulette had a simple but effective test: one had only to sample the Auschwitz air; the stench of burning bodies produced a nauseating odour that constantly hung over the camp.

One day there was an unexpected selection. For some it meant the slaughter-house, for it was time to weed out the weak and diseased. Each woman from Paulette's barracks would wait for her number with a mixture of fear and sorrow. It became impossible to ward off an insidious selfishness that made one almost happy to hear the numbers of other prisoners being read out, rather than one's own. There were seldom tears, only a bitter pain with a stranglehold on everyone. Paulette had survived. For that day at least.

When night came, there was little respite. Paulette's barracks, long and low, contained three levels of wooden bunks so tightly packed with occupants that when one wanted to turn, everyone else had to do likewise. Prisoners at Auschwitz were never made aware of any rules, but if one was broken, then they would most

147

often pay the ultimate price. Paulette soon learned that one of the more important of these unwritten rules was the absolute prohibition on turning one's head, whether during a roll-call, at work or even while in barracks.

Only occasionally were the rules spelled out with any clarity. One of the first that came to Paulette's attention was the customary SS jest:

'Here you enter by the door and exit through the chimney.'

It may well have seemed like a cruel Nazi jibe, but for most prisoners it was absolutely true. Various other phrases were inscribed on the walls of the barracks, including 'Halt dich sauber' (Keep yourself clean) and 'Eine Laus, dein Tod' (One louse and you're dead). Nor were these crude messages designed merely to coax, cajole, inform or advise. They were literally true. Worse still, since people were not provided with the means to keep themselves clean, breach of these cynical exhortations became an everyday, and potentially lethal, occurrence.

*   *   *

The truth about the remaining members of Convoy 55 was now quite clear. The trucks had made their way directly towards the gas chambers. There, loudspeakers explained that everyone was to be disinfected in the showers. To ensure that the doomed prisoners co-operated, this elaborate deception was maintained until the very end. Among the new arrivals there was above all a general feeling of relief and most were not distressed at the prospect of showering after their long and weary journey to the camp. They were ushered into a large room where the order was given to strip off completely and to make a neat pile of one's clothing, so that there would be no confusion when they were reclaimed. Bars of soap and a number of small towels were distributed.

The naked prisoners were then led towards the 'shower rooms,' where they were obliged to squeeze up close to one another. As the room began to fill, the SS would become increasingly agitated and brutal, hurling people in, brandishing their pistols and shouting wildly. Only now did panic set in. But it was too late.

The deception which had begun in Paris some three years earlier with the publication of the First Ordinance was now complete. Now the truth was there for everyone to see. The heavy doors were shut firmly. The attendant, wearing a gas-mask throughout, would wait a few moments while the temperature rose on account of the people packed inside. And then crystals of Zyklon-B were introduced. As soon as these made contact with the base of the pillars, poisonous fumes were released. Within minutes everyone was dead. It was as simple as that. If anyone remained in any doubt as to the reality of the 'Final Solution,' the answer was to be found at Auschwitz. It did not always happen in such an orderly fashion but the result was invariably the same, pile upon pile of bodies ending up in the furnaces. No one who entered a gas chamber was ever seen alive again.

Auschwitz had an astonishing capacity to massacre and maim; its ability to slaughter was unprecedented. Every day 10-12,000 people would be gassed to death; every day the camp's ten large crematoria were in operation. Viewing holes had been built into the walls of the gas chambers so that the SS or the occasional VIP from Berlin could see the unfolding of the awful scene inside. If one wanted to observe the 'Final Solution' in action, Auschwitz was the place.

After the gassing came the burning. The door on the far side of the gas chamber would be opened and the corpses loaded into a lift in order to be brought to the first floor, to the crematoria. Any who were not completely dead were thrown in with the rest. All of these tasks constituted the daily lot of the 'Sonderkommando,' a group made up almost exclusively of Jews who lived separately from the rest of the camp. They were provided with accommodation and nourishment superior to those of everyone else, for their work required muscle. But their usefulness was short-lived. Within weeks the entire group would itself be liquidated.

The corpses, still warm from the gas chamber, had to be examined. How many wedding rings were there? Which bodies contained teeth filled with gold? Was there any hair worth cutting again? Such were the issues that concerned the Sonderkommando.

As these helpless conscripts set about their macabre work, every item was collected by a section of the SS specifically created for this task. For the Sonderkommando there was no time to dwell on the enormity of what had just taken place; there was more work to be done. The bodies had to be loaded into the ovens and burned and the 'shower room' thoroughly cleaned. Finally, there were the ashes of the innocent victims to be disposed of. This entire operation had become so well rehearsed that it could be completed in under an hour. Time was of the essence. Train-loads of Jews were continuing to arrive. With the chambers soon ready for the next consignment, here was SS efficiency at its very best.

By the prevailing standards, Paulette Szlifke was well off and knew it. Together with her friends from Solidarité, she had been allocated to a 'Hausenkommando,' an 'outside' Kommando. It was the job of her group to begin draining a nearby swamp. Every morning, after roll-call, they would set off on foot through the main gate of the camp to the accompaniment of the women's orchestra, there to ensure a brisk pace in time with the cheerful march they provided. All around were the SS, bellowing out orders. If someone dropped dead while walking to the swamp, which often happened, the only consequence was an immediate order to move up closer to the person in front. It may have been a relative or friend, but to look round to see who had fallen was to risk death.

Half an hour later they would arrive at the swamp. Paulette's task was to fill and empty throughout the day a container with two handles at each end. This was no ordinary outdoor work, though: it had to be carried out at the double, while running from time to time across a narrow plank. Often, a girl would fall into the swamp. If that happened she was dead, not because the dank waters engulfed her, or because of a failed rescue attempt, but because in such cases the SS shot to kill.

A variety of games were played by the SS, and subtlety was not their most marked characteristic. For example, an SS officer might launch his cap into the distance and then instruct a prisoner to fetch it. Obliged to do precisely as instructed, she would immediately be shot. And the reason? The girl had just tried to escape, a capital offence.

With the completion of each day's work, the young women were ordered to carry back their dead co-workers: those who had fallen from the plank; those who had been sent to pick up the cap; and the others who had dropped from exhaustion, starvation or disease. The technique was always the same: two girls for every corpse, who were to station themselves to the rear of the returning Kommando. Sometimes these corpse-carrying girls would themselves be selected, for no apparent reason. So towards the end of each day's work there was a frantic rush to avoid this grim and hazardous task.

While Paulette survived the rigours of the 'swamp' Kommando, she eventually succumbed to the malaria that was rampant at Auschwitz. If one became ill, the last thing to do was to announce it. That would mean instant selection at the following morning's roll-call. So Paulette simply continued to report for work with the others, no matter how feverish she was, and in all weathers. But she was also well aware that in the daily battle for survival she was escaping death by the slenderest of margins.

The food, the constant obsession of the inmates, hardly helped. During the evening, when the bread was issued, there were those like Paulette who ate their ration straight away and others who preferred to save it for the morning. This seemingly prudent approach, however, usually meant an entire night awake, guarding the miserable offering. There was never enough to eat: a small portion of bread and margarine, with either a spoon of marmalade or a slice of salami. It was a starvation diet calculated to destroy.

In 1943, Yom Kippur fell in September, by which time Paulette had been at Auschwitz for a little over three months. The arrival of the Jewish High Holy Day did not make matters easier. By far the largest group in her Kommando was Polish girls who insisted on fasting, as was traditional. This presented an ideal opportunity for another SS game. Summoning Paulette's contingent, the guards inquired if anyone would like more soup since the Poles were not going to eat. It seemed a pity to let it go to waste. Naturally,

Paulette and her friends longed for extra rations, but refused to benefit from the religious convictions of their workmates. This was the response for which the SS had been waiting. The balance of the soup could now be poured into the swamp in full view of the emaciated prisoners.

Later that night, Paulette attempted to reason with the fasting Poles. Speaking in Yiddish, she tried to explain that in her view God would forgive them this small transgression. After all, another bowl of soup might mean another day's survival. Surely God would allow that? It was a dialogue with the deaf. The Polish reasoning was quite uncompromising: they retorted that it was precisely because of the likes of the French girls that God was now seeking to punish the Jews.

Another night. Strange, tinny voices could be heard from bunks above and below. For those like Paulette who sought peace and independence there was only one gateway to freedom: an escape into a world of fantasy. Paulette was a leader in this game. All that was required were imagination and belief:

'Who can make the most delicious meal?'

'You can? Go on then. What ingredients are you going to use? . . . No, surely not. You've got to add a good deal more sugar than that.'

'And what are we going to have tomorrow? All right, you can make the hors d'oeuvre, but tomorrow I'll be preparing the main dish.'

'I must say that tastes delicious. You must give me that recipe . . . Your mother, really?'

Another popular pastime was to return to Paris. It was such an easy journey:

'OK. Let's go from La République to Le Châtelet. Off you go.'

'Right, I'm going along the rue du Temple. Are you going that way?'

'No. I'm going to stick to the main boulevards. There's a lovely charcuterie just along the Boulevard de Sébastopol and I'm stopping in there now to get something for Madam Katan, my next-door neighbour.'

And when they tired of cooking and shopping, the evening could always be brought to a cultural conclusion with a concert.

'Oh, the Opera, it's such a wonderful building. Have you ever been there . . ?'

These brief excursions into the world of make-believe were often brought to an abrupt halt, however.

'Just a minute,' one of the girls would say, before the concert at the Opera had even started.

'Can you smell it?'

There would be a twitching of nostrils as the girls sought to sample that familiar odour. Yes, everyone could smell it. The smell was never far away. The crematoria had been working. They were always working. That day, another 10,000 Jews would have been gassed.

A day or two after Yom Kippur, Paulette and her four friends decided that they could take no more. Resolving not to return to the 'swamp' Kommando and aware that they would not have survived it much longer in any case, they resigned themselves to their fate. If they were to die within the camp, so be it. If their revolt led to the 'Himmel Kommando,' so be it. They were all half-dead anyway. But before abandoning hope completely they had cobbled together one desperate, last-ditch plan. The next morning, shortly after roll-call, they would attempt to escape from the 'swamp' Kommando. They knew that their chances of survival were extremely poor. Seldom did prisoners escape from Auschwitz. Five French teenagers were hardly likely to set a precedent. And yet each girl was prepared to risk her life. Early next morning, they would start to fight back.

*   *   *

Alone for a few moments on the platform of Weimar station, Armand Kohn reviewed the events of the four preceding days, during which time his family had undergone a drastic transformation. Still furious with Philippe for having dared to defy him, he then turned his anger on Rose-Marie. Not only had

153

she encouraged her brother to make the audacious leap from the train, she had actually joined him in that endeavour. But, most worrying of all, Armand had no idea what had become of them. The more he dwelled on the matter, the more he cursed himself for not having physically restrained them, for his greatest hope was for their safety and well-being.

It was at the station that the Kohn family was dispersed. Suzanne was taken off in one direction with Antoinette, while the youngest and eldest, Georges-André and Madame Marie-Jeanne, were ordered to take another train, its destination still unknown.

Most painful of all, though, was the fact that Armand Kohn himself now had to face some distressing truths. Not only had he been responsible for leading his wife, mother and children to their current plight, but his sole recourse during the long train journey had been to write a courteously-worded note, earnestly requesting that various notables in Paris be informed. Racked with guilt and shame, Armand Kohn was now left with no more than images of his shattered family. Georges-André. Philippe. Rose-Marie. Antoinette. Suzanne. Marie-Jeanne. Where were they now?

Armand was ordered to board another train. Only a short haul this time, but where? To Buchenwald. The setting of the concentration camp could hardly have been more picturesque. Whereas most camps were situated near towns that played little or no role in cultural history, Buchenwald was the notable exception. Erected in a quiet beech forest on the slopes of the Ettersberg, a hill closely linked with the German literary classics, the camp was set in picture-postcard land. Time and again in the letters of Goethe, Wieland and Schiller, the rolling slopes of the Ettersberg are mentioned. Here, where writers once strolled in search of inspiration, a concentration camp had been functioning for almost a decade. And over the camp's main gate, an inscription which perhaps said more than its author had intended:

Recht Oder Unrecht Mein Vaterland – 'My country right or wrong.'

The centre of a huge arms complex, Buchenwald may not have inflicted systematic extermination on a par with Auschwitz, but it had nonetheless exacted a sizeable toll. Inmates said that the thing to do on arriving at Buchenwald was to try to secure work in the munitions factory, for there one was apparently able to obtain a little more than the daily dose of watery soup and a chunk of dry bread.

If prisoners did not perish from starvation or disease, there was always the threat of being sent to the camp's mortuary block. Access to its lower level was by a steep stone staircase or a vertical chute below a trapdoor, down either of which prisoners would be precipitated for execution. Hanging was the most frequently used method of killing. Suspended on large iron hooks, some victims would take an hour to die. For stubborn prisoners who refused to expire fast enough, always to hand was the camp's heavy wooden club, with which the half-dead would be dealt a fatal blow.

By the time Armand Kohn arrived at Buchenwald, hundreds had died from a variety of other techniques, including injection of the typhus disease. Castration and sterilization by SS doctors were also everyday events in the camp's notorious 'medical wing.' Those who died were transported from the basement to the ground-floor crematorium in a large electric lift. In the yard outside, a series of carts would arrive regularly, each jammed with those who had perished from dysentery, disease or starvation. Inside the crematorium were a row of capacious arched ovens, each with a permanent jumble of calcined ribs, skulls and spinal columns.

Yet as Armand Kohn walked in through the camp's iron gate and towards the wooden barracks nearby, he retained the air of a bemused traveller; case in hand, nervously clutching as much clothing as possible, and wondering what sort of accommodation awaited him. Like every new inmate before him, he was struck by the striped, shaven-headed and skeletal figures all around. While the new intake awaited 'registration' at the camp, Armand occupied himself with his familiar collection of pens.

Armand was always ready to explain to anyone prepared to listen that each pen had a precise purpose: one for his secretary; another with which to settle accounts; one for correspondence, and so on. But within an hour, not only had he been robbed of his precious pens, he had also joined the ranks of the striped and shaven-headed. And then came the tattoo, right across the belly, so that there could be no mistake. Like Paulette Szlifke before him, Armand Kohn had become a number.

The one thing that would determine his continued existence or his progressive destruction, was the amount of time he would spend at Buchenwald. For, unlike Paulette, who had arrived at Auschwitz in June of 1943, Armand Kohn had been deported towards the very end of the war. Indeed, only a few hours before his arrival, Buchenwald had itself been bombarded. With the conflict in Europe drawing to a close, Armand Kohn felt confident that his stay at Buchenwald would be only a matter of weeks. Not for the first time, he was wrong. In fact, his survival could not be taken for granted. The liberation of Europe was still to be accomplished. But Buchenwald's process of destruction did not take long, averaging only twenty weeks.

Like Auschwitz, the camp had its eternal round of roll-calls, with the camp orchestra never far away, churning out marches. One of the senior officers used to derive great pleasure from being serenaded by tens of thousands of starving prisoners whose repertoire consisted of two songs, *The Castle in the Wood*, and the 'Buchenwald song.'

Within days, Armand had heard of Frau Ilse Koch, the wife of the former commandant of the camp. Hers was a reign that Kohn was fortunate to have missed. Known to inmates and staff alike as 'Frau Kommandant,' she enjoyed an awesome reputation for her penchant for lampshades and gloves made from the tattooed skin of dead inmates. She would personally select and have killed a prisoner with a particularly interesting or ornate tattoo. The skin would be carefully removed in the camp's pathology department and then presented to her. Ilse Koch enjoyed her time at Buchenwald so much that she chose to remain there for two years after her husband's removal following an investigation into his corruption.

The system of murder was often more systematic. Kohn soon learned that thousands of Russian prisoners of war had met their death at Buchenwald, murdered by the infamous *Genickschuss*. Believing they were to be medically examined, the captives were led into a large hall in which Germans in white coats ordered the men to strip down to the waist to be weighed. As each prisoner stood against a particular wall, a small-calibre pistol would be aimed at the back of his head through a hole. The trigger was pulled by an executioner standing the other side of the wall.

Loud recorded music would drown out the shots as soldier after soldier collapsed into a pile on the floor. Nor would any trace of blood remain, because the bullets had been specially designed not to exit via the other side of the skull. After the slaughter, sealed lorries would arrive to transport the bodies directly to the crematoria.

The destruction of Armand Kohn, deprived of any news concerning his family, was well advanced. Within a month or so of his arrival at Buchenwald, the former chief administrator had lost the will to live.

The camp's roll-call would take place twice daily in a huge square called the *Appelplatz*. In that square stood 'Goethe's Tree,' the only tree in the entire camp. According to legend, 'When that tree falls, so will the German empire.' Not surprisingly, the SS had left it standing. Desperate for news of his wife, mother and four children, and aware that time was not on his side, Armand Kohn now hoped and prayed that the tree would fall before long.

*   *   *

Paulette Szlifke's attempt to escape from the harshness of the 'swamp' Kommando was by no means well organized. Hers was not a secret world of meticulously drawn maps and painstakingly excavated tunnels. This was Auschwitz, the death camp; not Drancy, the detention centre. The five girls had agreed upon an idea which could scarcely have been more rudimentary: they were to make a run for it. As to precisely where they were going and what for, they really had only the vaguest of notions. The overriding goal was simply to get away before they too became the Kommando's unwitting victims.

157

It was time for the morning roll-call. Instead of presenting themselves in the customary fashion, the five girls set off in the opposite direction, strolling casually to begin with, but accelerating their pace as they realized that the moment they had talked of for so long appeared, as if spontaneously, to have arrived. As the roll-call was taking place in front of the barracks, Paulette and her friends hid behind the building, although it was hardly a hiding place at all. Those responsible for totting up the numbers noticed immediately that five of their contingent were missing – a fact hardly difficult to detect since an entire row was absent. Crouching precariously, Paulette sensed that the attempt to escape, lasting mere minutes, was over before it had even begun.

Instead of sounding the alarm, the two tellers, wanting to avoid a scene in which they themselves might be implicated, simply grabbed hold of the first five women who happened to be passing by. They urgently instructed them to join those still waiting to set off for the swamp, and the hastily reconstituted group marched towards the camp gates. It was as if nothing extraordinary had happened. Paulette and her friends exchanged looks, each girl's face revealing a slightly different mixture of silent relief and sheer incredulity.

They had succeeded in evading their Kommando, but what now? The only answer was to stray a little further. The five fugitives roamed from one building to another, mixing with those who remained in the camp and doing their utmost to look inconspicuous. Each girl was well aware that one false move and they would all be dead. Auschwitz offered grim alternatives to those caught attempting to escape: public hanging or the gas chamber.

However, so far so good. A few more buildings, a few more groups with which to mingle. Suddenly, the air was filled with the shrill blast of a whistle. Since the French girls had until now spent every one of their days outside the camp, no one knew what this meant. Seconds later, it could not have been more clear: another roll-call. All those who remained in the camp were to present themselves in front of their barracks to be counted yet again.

Within minutes the camp had swung into its familiar routine;

everybody, the old, the sick and the dying not excepted, emerged into the light. There was the usual round of shouting and shoving as those organizing the count conducted themselves at lightning pace. Paulette was in a panic. More urgent consultations within the group of five. There was only one thing for it: to head back to their own barracks. Anywhere else they would surely be revealed as interlopers.

As they made for their block, the girls sensed that this time they really were doomed. In front of the *Zugansblock*, the 'arrivals' block, stood all those legitimately entitled to remain in camp. Having presented herself in the immediate vicinity of her own quarters, had not Paulette in effect given herself up? Apparently not. For instead of her presence being questioned, she was ordered to go to another part of the camp. The five girls were fumbling their way around the camp and, for the moment at least, it appeared to be working.

Paulette and her friends remained unsure whether they had succeeded or not. On finding themselves in another section of the camp, they were forced to undergo the routine of their first few hours at Auschwitz: the removal of all clothing, and then a shower.

Paulette wondered if she had arrived at another centre of destruction of which she had been unaware. Perhaps there were more gas chambers. Certainly the Auschwitz complex was so large that few knew their way around it. But these were genuine showers. There followed the issue of a striped uniform, the hallmark of Auschwitz. Next, each girl was supplied with a red cap, which immediately distinguished them from the rest of the inmates.

Was this a good or a bad sign? Certainly the environment appeared much less menacing. They were then moved to a 'Coya,' slightly superior sleeping accommodation constructed in stone. It was there that they observed other identically clothed women, each bearing the distinctive red cap.

'You are in Canada,' whispered an anonymous voice a short distance away. The Canada in which Paulette had arrived was not the real Canada, with its resinous smell of pine trees. This was the Auschwitz version, smelling of the blood of murdered victims. 'Canada' was the inmates' nickname for the buildings in which prisoners' belongings, confiscated on arrival, were collected, sorted and distributed. Someone had given it the name, most probably because of the wealth and abundance supposed to exist in that country. Whatever its origins, the name had stuck.

Since the Jews had all along been informed that they were to be resettled in new homes, many had gone out of their way to ensure that their most precious of portable belongings accompanied them. The deception had been so effective that by the time Paulette arrived in the Canada Kommando, no fewer than thirty-five buildings were used for sifting through the vast quantities of property. She was to be one of the sifters. The accumulated wealth was as staggering as it was diverse, consisting of gold, currency, jewellery, diamonds, pearls, furs, clothes, eyeglasses, shoes, food, books, *objets d'art*, and piles of toys which had similarly been taken from their rightful owners.

The transportation of victims had become so frequent, and the systematic slaughter so widespread, that the riches had attained vast proportions. Except for those items which were appropriated on the spot by the SS guards, all gold and silver were sent in regular convoys to the bank of the German Reich. Watches went to the Central Office of Economic Administration of the SS at Oranienburg, and eyeglasses to the Department of Health. Objects of daily use such as handkerchiefs, knapsacks, bristle brushes, combs and the like, were taken to the office in charge of disseminating German culture. Temporarily stored in the barracks of Canada, goods were then despatched to Germany in a process that never stopped.

The traffic of Auschwitz was not exclusively one-way, for just as trains crammed with new victims were arriving daily at the camp's railway siding, so other trains were setting out with load after load of booty, headed westwards for the Reich. The entire operation was extremely well organized. Paulette, with her four friends, had been recruited to make that operation still more efficient. Berlin had indicated that this was work of the highest priority and that those working in the vast Canada Kommando were to be looked after.

By contrast with the 'swamp' Kommando, Paulette's new work always took place under shelter. Whereas the workers in the swamps were highly dispensable, the Canada Kommando's diverse range of valuables had to be protected from the Polish climate. Most of the girls who worked in Canada were pretty, clean and relatively well fed. From the perspective of the prisoner, the Canada Kommando was the élite corps of the camp. When representatives of the Red Cross eventually responded to international pressure and set off to inspect Auschwitz, it was the girls of Canada who were photographed and put on display.

Canada was good for the girls and good for the guards. Paulette soon realized that the SS went out of their way to ensure that the regime functioned smoothly, for the simple reason that most were preoccupied with pilfering. A silk blouse for a wife, jewellery for a mistress: there was never any shortage of luxury items from which to make a well-considered choice.

To Paulette, the way forward now appeared to be considerably clearer. As long as she did not stray from her newly allocated tasks, her chances of survival had increased immeasurably. Her ill-planned flight had turned out to be worthwhile. The entire atmosphere of Canada was a good deal more relaxed, too, with men present during working hours, some of them old friends from Paris. This mixing of the sexes boosted Paulette's spirits still further.

The colleagues from Solidarité lived up to the name and highest ideals of their movement. Within the Canada Kommando there existed an entire network of systems, backhanders, deals, contacts, and agreements that could be used to bolster one's chances of survival. And whereas the diet in the Canada Kommando was in principle the same as that of the rest of the camp, there was often to be found among the luggage the odd salami, a home-baked loaf, an onion or a potato. Naturally, the work was carefully supervised, but it nonetheless presented occasional opportunities to smuggle something out. The stakes were high for those who were caught, just as in any other quarter of the camp, but in Canada there at least existed a system that could be manipulated to the inmates' advantage.

Within the confines of the Canada Kommando, the classification of materials had become a highly specialized process. After the arrival of the trucks from the ramp where the 'selections' took place, the new haul would be pooled in a large yard. There would stand these privileged girls, ready to spring into action, each one given a specific task. Paulette's was to place every item of clothing that appeared to be in reasonable condition with other like items: shirts with shirts, jackets with jackets, and so on. The girls had strict instructions to look out for concealed valuables.

If an article of clothing was in unsatisfactory condition, its buttons, zips or studs were removed. Nothing was to be wasted. Meanwhile, other girls would take the bundles and stack them in other barracks nearby. Here, other groups carried out specific tasks: folding shirts, laundry style; folding underwear; stacking nightgowns, and so on. Each pile of clothing had to be made into neat packages of ten items and taken to a control point. Here, a piece of ribbon would be attached, along with the number of the bundler. A novel kind of quality control was employed: if there was any question concerning the bundle, it was simply necessary to make contact with the forearm of the particular bundler and inspect the tattoo to see if it matched.

Paulette Szlifke was but a cog in this enormous wheel, her task being known as *strapeling* – folding – men's jackets in particular. Compared to working in the swamp, the task could hardly have been easier. But even the folding had to be carried out in a precise and meticulous manner: the items were folded in half, shoulders together.

Only too aware of the fate of the owner of every jacket she folded, Paulette became reluctant to dwell on the matter. At Auschwitz one had a clear choice: to spend day and night churning over the horror stories, or to cut off from the aftermath of slaughter in which the Canada Kommando was so intimately involved. Paulette chose the latter, her ability to close her mind to the atrocities being one of the most valuable weapons in her armoury of survival. Yet there were those days when her protective veneer would simply fail the test.

One such day came in 1944, shortly after the arrival of a transportation from Hungary. That afternoon, Paulette's job was slightly different from usual. She and a few other members of the Canada Kommando had been instructed to go down to the railway lines to pick up a number of suitcases which, in the chaos of the selection process, had found their way onto the tracks. They then had to run back with the cases to the appropriate hangar. During one such shuttle a heavy case slipped from Paulette's arm and fell to the ground, evicting its contents. The chief occupant was a baby. It could not have been dead for long.

Recoiling with horror, Paulette pictured what must have happened: the distraught mother, alerted to the existence of the gas chambers, had chosen to end her baby's life with her own hands. Paulette attempted to rely on her familiar strategy: the grisly truth must not be allowed to sink in. Desperately, she tried to convince herself that what was before her was just another toy. Paulette knew precisely what to do: the little doll had to be picked up, tucked in, and put back to sleep again. But her capacity for self-deception simply refused to work. The suitcase was the cramped coffin of a tiny little life. That day there could be no running away. She could only grieve, pause, and then fight back. Paulette always fought back.

The centrepiece of the Canada Kommando was an enormous trunk into which all smaller items of value were poured – money and jewellery mainly. Aware that the contents of the trunk would end up in the coffers of the Reich, Paulette resolved to step up her small acts of resistance. So when the opportunity presented itself to destroy underfoot various pieces of paper money, or to crush a piece of jewellery, she would strike, despite the presence of SS guards all around.

The death of the baby was followed by the death of a close friend; there was death everywhere. If only those arriving could be informed of the horrors. They had to be warned and Paulette decided that she would at least attempt to do so. Maybe if they knew that their end was imminent they would rise up in revolt. With a friend scanning the Auschwitz terrain for guards, Paulette would every now and then venture from the confines of Canada and head for the camp's electrified fence. She had an urgent message for the new arrivals:

'Ce n'est pas une boulangerie,' the young girl would cry out. 'This is not a bakery, you know.'

She spoke in French, Yiddish, Polish – anything to get through to the new intake of innocents.

Those new arrivals who noticed the small striped figure on the other side of the enclosure would look at her vacantly.

'For God's sake,' Paulette would shriek, 'For God's sake – do something.'

More blank looks.

'You are going to be burned. Gassed. You are going to be killed. Do something.'

The new arrivals continued to look on in disbelief. Every now and then, though, someone would respond. Had her words been heeded?

'What are you talking about, you little fool? Can't you see this is a factory?'

The voice had come from somewhere within the crowd. The weary travellers would point to the large chimneys as proof that they had arrived at some kind of industrial complex.

It was no use. People were not listening. Some had even jeered. One last try:

'Please, I beg you, people . . . do something. This isn't a laundry or factory . . . for God's sake – your relatives, your families are being burned here.'

But pleased now to have an opportunity of stretching their legs, they continued on their way. Only one thing was on their minds: the sooner their resettlement began, the better.

Paulette would return to her Canada quarters. Certainly she was lucky not to have been caught, but she despaired nonetheless. The truths she had bellowed through the perimeter fence had been so unpalatable, so unbelievable, that they had been completely ignored. Still, she would try again the following day should an opportunity present itself. At Auschwitz you could be certain that more trains would arrive. Paulette hoped and prayed that soon someone might listen.

Epilogue:

Survivors, Strippel and Syria

The concentration camps of Auschwitz and Buchenwald were just two of several Nazi centres of slaughter and destruction. France was just one of several countries from which the camps received their victims. What distinguished France from other occupied countries? Above all, the fact that she had a long-established liberal and democratic tradition. Indeed, for many years, France had been a haven for Jews fleeing from the oppression of eastern Europe. True, anti-Semitism existed in certain sections of French society, as the Dreyfus case had demonstrated only too vividly fifty years earlier. But the violent press campaigns and street clashes witnessed during that 'affaire' were mild compared with anti-Jewish sentiment in Poland, long known for her endless pogroms and persecutions.

Moreover, at the start of the German occupation in June of 1940, France was home to the largest Jewish community in the entire western arc. The Jewish population had reached a total of 270,000, almost three quarters of whom were living in the Paris area. From the early arrival of Helmut Knochen in the French capital, right through to the departure of Aloïs Brünner some four years later, the one objective about which there was seldom any disagreement was the desire to liquidate France's Jewish community.

Did the Nazis succeed? Strictly speaking, no. The Jews of France were not wiped out. Today there are at least three quarters of a million Jews in France and the ancient Jewish quarters of Le Sentier and Belleville, in Paris, are as busy as ever before. So what price the 'Final Solution' in France? A very high price indeed. The Germans may not have succeeded in eradicating all Jews from French soil, but they made a serious attempt to do so. Eichmann may not have been satisfied, but French Jewry was maimed and mauled beyond all recognition.

In total, the Germans succeeded in deporting more than 75,000 Jews from France. The most typical route was from Drancy to the death camp of Auschwitz where immediate gassing awaited the vast majority. Of those deportees who survived the process of 'selection,' fewer than 2,700 returned, less than four per cent. All of these were adults. No child ever found his or her way back to France. If those who died on French soil are included, at least 80,000 French Jews were victims of the 'Final Solution.'

Seventy-five thousand. Eighty thousand. Five million Jews. Six million Jews. Can anyone begin to grasp the meaning of these anonymous statistics? Certainly, if anyone wants to inspect the long lists of those deported, each name is there in a book the size of a weighty telephone directory.

While the death toll of French Jews is easy enough to quantify, the scale of human suffering is far more difficult to assess. The truth is that it cannot properly be done. For unless the plight of every one of those 80,000 is described in detail, no one will ever know the full extent of their suffering. Two of the names on those long lists of deportees are those of Armand Kohn and Paulette Szlifke. Armand's name is next to the six other members of his family. What became of these eight people – eight from 80,000? Four returned. Four did not.

Suzanne and Antoinette Kohn

Armand's wife and eldest daughter both perished at the concentration camp of Bergen-Belsen. When they arrived at Belsen, it was to all intents and purposes a starvation camp. Well dressed and elegantly made-up, despite the hardships of their ordeal in the cattle-car, neither survived for long. Both women suffered at the hands of other inmates. Within days everything had been stolen from them, including their bed-covers. Unused to, and incapable

assume that they had perished at Auschwitz. It was impossible to confirm. In one case he was right; in the other he was not.

Far from attacking their father for his stubbornness, and for having led them to their predicament in which they, too, suffered and grieved, Philippe and Rose-Marie Kohn rallied around him, giving him all the support they could muster. For Armand had become so diminished as a man, and so physically ill, as a result of his disastrous attempt to remain in Paris throughout the war, that it had become almost unthinkable to do otherwise. Certainly, it would have served no useful purpose, and so his two children sought not to burden him further.

Others were less sensitive, taking pleasure in reminding Armand how ironic it was that it was he who had led his family to the camps and yet it was he, not they, who had returned. Such statements may have been stripped of all tact and diplomacy, but Armand was quite unable to counter those who sought to torment him.

As Armand slumped into ill-health, a Danish nurse was hired to help look after him in his grief. She was the first woman with whom Armand had had any contact for a number of years and he eventually married her.

Riddled with guilt, Armand constantly bemoaned the fact that he had not perished himself. At first, he would repeatedly ask why could he not have been killed and his family spared. But in time, his eternal question unanswered, the subject of the war years grew so painful that it became taboo. For Armand Kohn, the most satisfactory solution appeared to be to say nothing. Four of his family who had accompanied him on that last train journey had not returned. He had had every opportunity to leave France but had consistently declined to do so. He had received guidance from every quarter, first only advising him, but eventually pleading with him to leave. And still he had declined. Even the Kohns' cruel nickname – 'the volunteers of death' – had failed to persuade him to budge. With his family now in tatters, and Armand himself drowning in unfathomable depths of remorse, what was there to say?

On April 11, 1945, Allied bulldozers finally destroyed Buchenwald's solitary tree. The legend surrounding 'Goethe's Tree' had been proved correct. But for Armand Kohn the felling of that tree had come too late. The German empire had already robbed him of four members of his own family.

Armand Kohn died in Paris on June 18, 1962.

Georges-André Kohn

Most of the French deportees who survived the Holocaust were repatriated in the spring of 1945. A Paris hotel, the Lutetia, became the unofficial registration centre for survivors. Relatives and friends would go there to scan the lists of those known to have been liberated. When the names of loved ones could not be found on the lists, as was most often the case, relatives were to be seen wandering around the hotel, showing photographs, wedding pictures, or snapshots, desperate for news. Within weeks, the walls of the Lutetia were covered with identity cards, many belonging to children, each document bearing the particulars of somebody who had yet to return and whose name did not appear on any list.

One of those identity cards belonged to Georges-André Kohn, twelve years old in 1945 and the youngest of Armand's four children. The former chief of the Rothschild Hospital launched a desperate search for his little boy. Before long he had succeeded in making contact with Auschwitz survivors who had seen his son there. They reported that Georges-André had survived the selection process, but they knew little else besides.

Armand decided there was little he could do. In the absence of information to the contrary, he was forced to presume that Georges-André had perished at Auschwitz. It was hardly an astonishing conclusion, for the corridors of the Lutetia reverberated with thousands of tragic tales. For Armand Kohn it was the loss of the fourth member of his family in as many weeks.

Time passed, and Georges-André never returned. Before long the French government issued an official death certificate bearing the words 'Mort pour la France.' According to this document, the little boy had sacrificed his short life for his country. Such was the version of events which prevailed for almost thirty-five years after the war. It was only in 1979, seventeen years after Armand's death, that the truth about Georges-André finally began to emerge.

The young boy had indeed been at Auschwitz, at the *Arbeitslager*; Camp D, to be precise. He had arrived at the death camp in the typically stylish attire of the Kohn family, wearing a white shirt, grey flannel trousers, and navy-blue blazer and carrying a small suitcase in his right hand. The survivors to whom Armand had spoken at the Lutetia had been correct in reporting that Georges-André had survived the selection process, itself something quite remarkable for a young child.

Aware that his mother was in the women's barracks situated opposite his own, the boy succeeded at first in smuggling letters to her through the secret network of the camp's resistance. After six weeks, though, the letters stopped. As the little boy became increasingly weak and dispirited, he realized that his ailing health meant that he risked being selected for the gas chambers. As the Polish winter of 1944 began to bite, Georges-André was sent to work out in the open, wheeling around a cargo of either rubbish or wood on a little trolley.

On November 27, 1944, Georges-André's German *Kapo* (a prisoner given authority by the Germans) instructed him to abandon his work. A special journey had been arranged, with twenty children earmarked to set off from the camp. Travelling in a special wagon forming part of a regular passenger train, the children were to pass as typhoid carriers, in order to explain their isolation. As the train approached the outskirts of Berlin, Georges-André looked out towards the capital of the Reich and whispered to the youngster next to him that if he only had somewhere to go, he would dearly love to run away.

The destination of this unconventional convoy was the concentration camp of Neuengamme, just outside Hamburg. Upon arrival Georges-André assumed that perhaps he was indeed sick, because he immediately found himself installed in the camp's 'hospital' wing. Compared with the conditions of Auschwitz, the camp of Neuengamme at first appeared to be rather luxurious. There was absolutely no work to do, the supply of food was ample, and there appeared to be many people to attend to his needs. There was even heating within Georges-André's wing, especially welcome after the bitter Polish winter.

The truth about Neuengamme, though, was entirely different. The twenty children had been transferred from Auschwitz for a particular purpose. They were to be human guinea-pigs in a series of medical experiments conducted under the auspices of a certain Dr Kurt Heissmeyer. From a family of pro-Nazi medical staff, he had long embraced the familiar ideology that held that since Jews were inferior beings, any experiments carried out on them were equivalent only to those performed on animals.

So it was that Georges-André underwent a series of injections and incisions, his body being filled with germs from a variety of diseases, most specifically those of tuberculosis. The condition of all the children deteriorated very rapidly. Unable to leave the barracks at any time, Georges-André became the weakest and most apathetic of the entire group. The nurses participating in the experiments were eventually obliged to physically transport the little boy to different barracks in which radiography and follow-up examinations took place. Day and night Georges-André remained confined to his bed, unable to leave it even during the increasingly frequent air-raids on Hamburg.

With British troops approaching the city and cannon fire in the distance, the Germans knew that the time for their experiments was expiring rapidly. Suddenly, priorities changed, the first of these being how to cover up their crimes. On April 20, 1945, the day on which Adolf Hitler was celebrating his fifty-sixth birthday, SS-Obersturmführer Arnold Strippel, the head of all those Kommandos annexed to the concentration camp of Neuengamme, gave the order for all the children to be hanged, along with twenty-four Russian prisoners of war.

The twenty youngsters, some of whom were only five years old, were informed that they were being transferred to the camp of Theresienstadt. The youngest of the children clutching their toys, they were in fact driven from Neuengamme to the school of Bullenhuser Damm, part of Strippel's domain. A large disused building in the Rothenburg quarter of Hamburg, this had sustained extensive damage during the Allied onslaught on the city two years earlier. The children were taken to the basement of the school where an SS 'doctor' by the name of Trzebinski injected them with morphine. The children were ordered to undress and then hanged.

Such were the circumstances of the death of Georges-André Kohn. Subjected to a monstrous programme of bogus medical experiments, he was murdered within a few hours of the liberation of Neuengamme. He was murdered four days before April 23, 1945, the day on which he would have been celebrating his bar mitzvah.

Of the seven members of the Kohn family who set off on Aloïs Brünner's last convoy, only Philippe remains alive today. On discovering the true facts of his young brother's death, Philippe's reaction was one of unrestrained grief and horror.

But he then suffered a shock that was possibly even greater: the fact that Arnold Strippel, the most senior officer who had given the order for the execution of Georges-André, was alive and well in Germany, as he still is today. The owner of an elegant villa situated on the outskirts of Frankfurt, and the recipient of a state pension, Arnold Strippel has still to be found responsible for the crimes committed at Bullenhuser Damm.

Philippe Kohn has therefore been unable to close the door on the suffering of his family, for he is now actively involved in a campaign to prosecute Strippel. There has been an endless series of lawsuits, demonstrations, remonstrations, lobbying, even a sympathetic letter from the Private Office of the President of the French Republic. Now, almost ten years after the crimes of Bullenhuser Damm were uncovered, the case against Strippel is unlikely ever to be brought before a court of law.

On June 19, 1981, Philippe Kohn succeeded in obtaining a new death certificate in respect of his brother. He had not 'died for France,' as the first piece of paper had put it. An official document issued this time by the German authorities is a little more explicit: Georges-André Kohn 'died during the night of April 20–21, 1945.'

With the case against Strippel making virtually no progress at all, Philippe Kohn, together with other relatives of the children who perished, formed an organization called 'The Children of Bullenhuser Damm.' On April 20, 1986, exactly forty-one years after the murders, the members staged a symbolic trial attended by a number of prominent jurists. At the conclusion of the hearings and having reviewed all the evidence, the tribunal established 'the guilt of Arnold Strippel.' The official tribunals of Hamburg, however, have yet to do likewise.

Paulette Szlifke

In January of 1945 the Russians were edging towards Auschwitz, while the German army was retreating on all fronts, leaving a trail of fire and destruction in its wake. Desperately, the Nazis attempted to conceal the evidence of mass murder, pulling up railway lines to the camps and dismantling equipment. Aware that the apparatus of genocide would have to be destroyed, they blew up the gas chambers and crematoria of Auschwitz. But what to do with the 66,000 prisoners who so far had eluded death?

Paulette Szlifke was one among that number. Her escape from the swamps and into the more privileged world of the Canada Kommando had been largely responsible for her continued survival. She had been at the death camp for almost two years.

In the face of the continuing Soviet advance, Berlin ordered that the entire population of the camp be evacuated back towards the heartland of Germany. Those too sick or too old to move, about ten per cent of the prisoners, remained at Auschwitz. For Paulette and her colleagues from Solidarité, a new dilemma arose: to stay or to go? At least she had come to know the lie of the land, and knew as much about the camp as any inmate. There was another

arm. And after she has spoken, whether publicly or privately, about her experiences at the hands of both the Germans and the French, she grieves for some days, the old wounds having been reopened.

For Paulette, the days are one thing; the nights quite another. Her recurrent nightmare is always a variation on the same theme: she is arriving at Auschwitz, everything is being taken from her, her clothes, her hair, her possessions – everything. By the time she wakes, either in the middle of the night or in the early hours, Paulette Sarcey has quite unconsciously removed the rings from her fingers. Above all else, she is haunted by the eyes of small children, some of whom are barely able to walk, children who are filled with terror, somehow able to sense the fate which awaits them. So Paulette Sarcey is a survivor. But to this day she is not free.

*   *   *

Damascus 1989

Damascus is the oldest city in the world. Boasting a history that goes back to the days of Abraham, the city still presents a splendid spectacle. George Haddad Street is one of the city's many quiet, tree-lined thoroughfares in which scores of pensioners have chosen to end their days. Tucked away in the Abu Rumaneh district of the city, George Haddad Street contains one particular block which adjoins another road, Abdel Madek Street. This drab building, covered for the most part in off-yellow paint, greets entrants with a double gate of wrought iron and a list of names next to doorbells. One name is missing. It is that of the old man who lives on the third floor. Although Georg Fischer is well known to his neighbours, the seventy-six-year-old retired Austrian who lives there has come to the conclusion that it would not be in his best interests to disclose his identity to the world.

Before long, it becomes apparent that there is something quite unusual about Georg Fischer. For just opposite those undistinguished wrought-iron gates, there stands each day a tall young man with a zipped-up black leather jacket and a pistol in his belt. At each end of the street there is usually an additional security man.

If old Mr Fischer therefore appears to be an unconventional pensioner, he is most certainly that. For to at least one close friend he has confided that Georg Fischer is in fact Aloïs Brünner, the former SS-Hauptsturmführer responsible for the deportation of 150,000 Austrian, German, Greek, French and Czechoslovakian Jews.

Aloïs Brünner was the man responsible for sending Paulette Szlifke to Auschwitz. And he was the former Drancy chief who went to great lengths to deport Armand Kohn, together with his entire family. Could it possibly be that Aloïs Brünner is alive and well in Syria today? Unthinkable? Certainly not.

Unlike his aide Bruckler, Brünner decided not to embark upon the last train out of the Paris area. Heading back towards Germany in an ordinary Citroën, Eichmann's most trusted lieutenant first resurfaced in Czechoslovakia. With Drancy liberated the day after Brünner's departure from France, it was more than clear to the majority of the SS that the war was over. But not for Aloïs Brünner. His war against the Jews had still to run its course. Posted to head the camp of Sered, he was able to add the names of another 13,000 deportees – this time Slovakian Jews – to his awesome total.

Within a year of the end of hostilities, the French authorities had issued a warrant for Brünner's arrest. Eight years later Brünner was sentenced to death by a French military court. But the sentence was pronounced *in absentia*, for Brünner had long since fled those areas of Europe where he was most vulnerable.

During the early 1950s Brünner surfaced once again, this time in Egypt. With the help of the former General Otto Ernst Remer and a third man in West Germany, they together set up Otraco, the Orient Trading Company, which dealt, often illegally, in arms. Just as American intelligence recruited Klaus Barbie for espionage work in early 1947, so the Central Intelligence Agency bankrolled the activities of Brünner during his stay in Egypt in 1953. The full story of US intelligence relations with Brünner, however, remains shrouded in mystery – and is likely to stay so for some time, since both Brünner and the CIA have not surprisingly gone out of their way to ensure that such matters remain out of the public domain. Before long, Brünner and Remer had moved on again, to Damascus, where Brünner wasted no time in making himself helpful to the then Syrian President, Amin Hafez. By this time Brünner had adopted the alias of Georg Fischer, which he has retained to this day. In fact, Brünner instructed the Syrian security forces in the use of an ingenious mechanical aid to interrogation. It was a wheel upon which prisoners could be strapped and beaten with a length of electric cable. Every few minutes, an automatic pump would spray water through the wheel to open the prisoner's wounds, after which beatings could resume.

In 1960, with those countries seeking him still unable to identify his whereabouts, Brünner was continuing to give occasional assistance to the Syrian authorities, this time advising on the purchase of 2000 items of bugging equipment from East Germany. Two years later Brünner was named in connection with a plot to kill the president of the World Jewish Congress, Nahum Goldman. He was alleged to have sent a Lebanese citizen to Vienna to organize the assassination, but West German security agents intervened and a number of West German neo-Nazis were implicated.

Since his retreat from Europe, Brünner has been separated from his wife Anni and his daughter Irene, although he has maintained contact with both. In 1969, Irene Brünner married Bertram Haller, the holder of a doctorate in law. Their wedding took place in Vienna. Frau Anni Brünner, although still officially married to her husband, now shares her life with a retired police inspector by the name of Joseph Kirtschl.

As the years of freedom turned into decades, Brünner became ever more certain that he had eluded a conviction for war crimes. In 1981, however, the former SS chief received a verdict from an altogether unofficial tribunal. When a parcel arrived bearing the familiar postmark of Vienna, Brünner assumed that it was from his family, who still live in the Austrian capital. But the package contained a significant quantity of explosives, which detonated on opening. No one knows who was responsible, although the bomb was most probably an initiative of the Israeli intelligence service, Mossad. Whatever the parcel's origin, it did what it had been intended to do, for Brünner lost four fingers from his left hand and sustained damage to his eyes.

It was only in June of the following year that the hunt for Aloïs Brünner began to make serious progress. This was due almost entirely to the efforts of Maître Serge Klarsfeld, the Paris-based lawyer whose reputation as a Nazi-hunter is well known. Quite apart from acting in his capacity as chairman of the association of those taking civil action against Brünner, Serge Klarsfeld had a personal debt to settle. Brünner had been responsible for deporting Serge's father, Arno, during his reign of terror at Drancy. Having flown to Syria to protest against Brünner's presence there, Klarsfeld was promptly turned back at Damascus airport. Given a government whose official position was to deny the very existence of Georg Fischer, something most peculiar had happened. During the forty-eight hours following Klarsfeld's brief visit, three car-loads of Syrian security men were stationed outside Brünner's apartment in George Haddad Street.

This public 'demasking' of Georg Fischer has in turn led to a flurry of legal activity in a number of countries around the world. Now, the governments of Greece, France, West Germany, East Germany, Israel, Czechoslovakia and Austria have all initiated proceedings, some with more enthusiasm than others, in an attempt to bring Brünner to justice. Wherever Brünner set foot in his career within the ranks of the SS, there is now a warrant out for his arrest or an action for extradition pending. Maître Klarsfeld remains the driving force behind the greater part of these manoeuvres, but so far they have all been to no avail. Every now and then a report filters through that Brünner is about to be extradited from Syria. Yet an extradition has always failed to materialize. The reason is invariably the same: so far as the Syrian government is concerned, Aloïs Brünner does not exist.

One year after Serge Klarsfeld's brief encounter with Syrian soil, a British journalist, Robert Fisk of *The Times*, visited Damascus in an attempt to meet Brünner. When asked if Aloïs Brünner was in Damascus, an official government spokesman confirmed the Syrians' long-standing line:

'I have made inquiries and we have no such man in Syria.'

Fisk eventually managed to make contact with the man known as Georg Fischer. His brusque refusal when asked to discuss his role during the war hardly came as a surprise:

'No. I cannot do so. I have signed an agreement with the Syrian Government never to give any interviews.'

Three years later Brünner broke his self-imposed silence. In 1985, the Munich-based weekly magazine *Bunte* landed a scoop. Two reporters spoke at length with Eichmann's ex-aide. The magazine was full of pictures of the former SS man strolling the streets of Damascus. As for his war-time record:

I'm prepared to go on trial before an international court of law and justify my acts. Only Israel won't get me. I won't become a second Eichmann.

Bunte went on to report that Brünner had showed his two interviewers a suicide capsule that never leaves his possession, in case Israeli agents try to kidnap him.

In 1987, forty-two years after the end of the Second World War, Interpol finally agreed to conduct their own search. The most recent recruit in the campaign to bring Aloïs Brünner to justice is in many respects the most ironic. For Kurt Waldheim, the President of the Austrian Republic, whose own war record has come under much scrutiny, publicly called for Brünner's extradition during the course of an official visit to Damascus.

Aloïs Brünner is now the last and most important war criminal still at large. Perhaps the most striking feature of his continued freedom is that everyone knows precisely where he is and the nature of his crimes. And while Eichmann must surely retain the dubious acclaim as the world's foremost bureaucratic murderer, his chief aide has blood on his hands in a far more immediate sense. Whereas Eichmann was happy to rattle out the orders, it was invariably Aloïs Brünner who ensured that they were carried out. Indeed, at the Nuremberg trials Brünner was described as 'the most cold-blooded killer in Eichmann's retinue.' Of course Eichmann had a rather different perception of Brünner's role, describing him as 'one of my best men.'

Brünner's first convoy from France was the one in which Paulette Szlifke made her arduous journey to the East. His last convoy contained all seven members of Armand Kohn's family. Yet Brünner remains unpunished for either of these crimes, or for any one of the deaths of the tens of thousands of men, women and children deported between the two convoys. In fact the Simon Wiesenthal Center in Los Angeles estimates that Brünner is personally responsible for the murder of 128,500 people. With writs, warrants, extraditions and an assortment of other legal actions making little headway, Aloïs Brünner remains free, never having set foot in any court of law under any jurisdiction on any charge of any description.

A trial cannot bring back Antoinette Kohn. Nor Suzanne Kohn. Nor Armand's mother, Marie-Jeanne. A trial cannot rewrite history and undo the atrocities inflicted on the little boy, Georges-André. Nor would the extradition of Aloïs Brünner enable Paulette Szlifke to sleep more easily. And there is the distinct possibility that Aloïs Brünner will die before any of the numerous legal processes now in hand ever succeeds in catching up with him.

Aloïs Brünner has no regrets about his role in the 'Final Solution.' In the *Bunte* interview, he stressed that he felt not the slightest remorse or sorrow about his treatment of the Jews. On the contrary, his role had been quite simple. In his own words he had only been 'getting rid of that rubbish.' In November of 1988, in a brief telephone conversation with a journalist from the *Chicago Sun-Times*, Brünner reaffirmed his hatred of the Jews: 'The Jews who were exterminated deserved to die because they were agents of the Devil and human rubbish,' adding: 'I have no regrets whatsoever and if I had my time again I'd do exactly the same.' This was Brünner's message, possibly his last, to those slaughtered as a consequence of his actions. To the 46,091 Jews from the Greek city of Salonika; to the 75,000 Jews deported from

France; to Paulette Szlifke, and to each member of the Kohn family – all rubbish, each and every one of them.

The diary of an SS doctor

The Holocaust is well documented by survivors and historians alike. For the moment, at least, there appears to be no shortage of people like Paulette Szlifke, prepared to relate stories of personal suffering to the widest possible audience. But every now and then a piece of more unconventional evidence appears. Such was the case with the discovery of the diary kept by one Obersturmführer Johann Kremer. A professor of anatomy at the University of Munich, he was appointed to the camp of Auschwitz on August 30, 1942. His arrival is mentioned in the Auschwitz Notebooks. On September 2, at three in the morning, he attended an execution by gas for the first time. The victims were Jews who had been deported from France. Of the 957 people arriving from Drancy, only twelve men and twenty-seven women succeeded in surviving the selection process. The 918 Jews who remained, all of them arrested during *La Grande Rafle* some six weeks earlier, were left for execution. This wholesale massacre of innocent men, women and children prompted the SS doctor to make the following entry in his diary:

> At 3 am, I watched for the first time a 'special action.' By comparison Dante's Hell seems to me to be something of a farce.

And yet Johann Kremer was not sufficiently distracted by the proceedings to be unable to make an additional entry in his journal for that same day:

> Because of the exhausting work they had had to do, the SS who took part in this operation were issued with supplementary rations of a fifth of a quart of alcohol, five cigarettes, a fifth of a pound of sausage, and one extra ration of bread.

Such was the world of Auschwitz. When small groups of survivors from France gather together, as they sometimes do, they invariably arrive at the same conclusion: that there really are no words to describe the suffering and hopelessness of Auschwitz. Arrange the words in any manner and it will remain quite impossible to capture its evil and inhumanity. It is easy enough to say, 'Auschwitz was Hell.' But who can really imagine Hell without having been there?

INDEX

INDEX